T0302498

create dream catchers

Create Dream Catchers
First published in the United States in 2021 by Stash Books, an imprint of C&T Publishing, Inc.,
P.O. Box 1456, Lafayette, CA 94549

Original Korean edition published by Cheong Publishing Ltd., Paju-si, Korea.
English language rights, translation & production by World Book Media, LLC.

Publisher: Sung-Woo Park
Editor: Ji-Hae Kim
Design: Hae-Jin Jung
Translator: Yoon-Kyung Chang
English Language Editor: Lindsay Fair

ISBN: 978-1-64403-128-5

Manufactured in China
10 9 8 7 6 5 4 3 2 1

create dream catchers

26 Serene Projects to Crochet,
Weave, Macramé & More

Young-Ran Lee

stashBOOKS®
ctpub.com

CRÈME

Contents

Introduction 7 • The Origin of the Dream Catcher 11
Tools & Materials 12

Theme 1: Protection 17

Dream Catcher Bag Charm 18
Dream Catcher Necklace 19

Theme 2: Beauty 23

Flower Bouquet Dream Catcher 24
Flower Vine Dream Catcher 26

Theme 3: Individuality 33

Triangle Dream Catcher 34
Vertical Net Dream Catcher 36

Theme 4: Good Fortune 41

Sea Glass Dream Catcher 42
Summer Dream Catcher 44

Theme 5: Grace 49

Lace Dream Catcher 50
Miniature Flower Dream Catcher 51

Theme 6: Patience 55

Camping Dream Catcher 56
Dream Catcher Garland 58

Theme 7: Prayers 63

God's Eye 64
God's Eye Wall Hanging 68

Theme 8: Clarity 71

Bird Wreath Dream Catcher 72
Bird Perch Dream Catcher 76

Theme 9: Nature 79

Sunshine Dream Catcher 80
Mystical Dream Catcher 84

Theme 10: Heritage 87

Woven Net Dream Catcher 88
Tapestry Dream Catcher 90

Theme 11: Blessings 97

Dream Catcher of Hope 98
Shades of Green Dream Catcher 100

Theme 12: Health 105

Dream Catcher Mobile 106
Pyramid Dream Catcher Mobile 108

Theme 13: Serenity 115

Air Plant Dream Catcher 116
Plant Hanger Dream Catcher 118

Inspiration Gallery 124
Crochet Stitch Guide 140
Resources 142
About the Author 144

Introduction

It's November, around the time when we're about to have the first snowfall of the season. I tighten the shoelaces on my trekking boots and head out for an early morning hike. If I were to bump into a stranger during my hike, I wouldn't be surprised if they were frightened by my appearance—my hat is pulled down low over my eyes to protect me from the cold and I am carrying a huge pair of pruning shears in one hand.

This is the best time of year to find branches for making dream catchers—the leaves have fallen off the trees and I can venture through the woods without worrying about snakes since they're hibernating. My arms and legs may get covered in scratches and my fingers may get pricked by thorns, but when I descend from the mountain with my arms full of tree branches that will be reborn as dream catchers, I feel as proud as a farmer who has just finished fall harvest.

Collecting the supplies from Mother Nature may involve a bit of hard work, but as you weave the strands of yarn or twine together, with the recipient's happiness and serenity in mind, the dream catcher you are creating transforms into the most divine and precious gift.

I wish these dream catchers provide you with peaceful slumber and ease your worries when you lay your head down to rest after a day's work.

I wish these dream catchers inspire hopeful dreams to your heart's content.

I wish the dream catchers offer solace to your family and friends.

And I wish this book is helpful for those interested in creating handmade dream catchers from the heart.

—Young-Ran Lee

The Dream Catchers

The Origin of the Dream Catcher

A dream catcher is a handmade ornament designed to catch nightmares and bring pleasant dreams. It originates from Native American culture, most likely from the Ojibwa people of the Great Lakes region.

There are several origin stories related to the tradition of dream catchers. One Ojibwa legend attributes the origin of dream catchers to Asibikaashi, or Spider Woman, the spiritual guardian of the tribe's children. According to the story, Asibikaashi could easily protect all the children and babies in the early days of the Native American people, but as the population increased and the tribes expanded to faraway lands, it became difficult for her to make the journey across such a large area. As a result, the women of the Ojibwa tribe began making dream catchers to protect their sleeping children.

The Ojibwa believe that the dream catcher's web traps nightmares until they can be purified by the morning sunlight. Other tribes believe that nightmares pass through, while only happy dreams remain in the web and travel down the dream catcher's feather and into the minds of those sleeping underneath.

Regardless of the tribe, all origin stories share the same belief that dream catchers bring sweet dreams.

Nearly every element of a dream catcher has meaning. The characteristic round shape symbolizes the sun and the moon, and their movement in the sky. The woven threads are patterned after a spider's web. Feathers provide a soft ladder for pleasant dreams to float down and gently enter into the mind. A single bead may represent the spider that created the web, while multiple beads may represent good dreams that could not pass through the web and were immortalized in the form of sacred charms.

The symbolism of the dream catcher varies based on the unique beads and feathers used. For example, turquoise is believed to bring success and victory, while amethyst represents health and peace. Owl feathers, which symbolize wisdom, were often used for girls, while eagle feathers, which signify bravery, were often used for boys.

In Native American culture, dreams offer entrance into another realm, one beyond reality. It is believed that dreams provide spiritual guidance and wisdom, so making and giving dream catchers conveys a beautiful and heartfelt message of hope and comfort for the recipient.

Tools & Materials

You don't need lots of fancy supplies for making dream catchers. In fact, the most beautiful materials can be found in nature. Enjoy taking walks through the woods or along the beach and collect branches, feathers, and shells along the way. You'll also need some twine, yarn, and beads to add color and texture to your designs. Always opt for natural materials for the best results.

Materials

1. Branches
Look for flexible branches, such as grapevines, willow, wild rosebush, and forsythia, that can be bent into shape to make dream catcher frames. Straight branches can also be used—connect several to form a tapestry frame.

2. Waxed twine
Use coated hemp or cotton twine to secure the frames and to weave the dream catcher webs. Waxed twine is very durable and is available in a variety of colors and thicknesses.

3. Beads
Opt for beads made from natural materials, such as stones, seashells, animal bones, coconut shells, nuts, and seeds. Carved wooden beads are available in various sizes, colors, and shapes, including circles, tubes, and ovals.

4. Feathers
Natural feathers that have been sterilized are widely available through millinery and costume supply shops. The designs in this book use ostrich, peacock, pheasant, and hawk feathers among others. You can also find bird feathers on nature walks.

5. Yarn
Use natural fiber yarn, such as cotton, wool, and linen, to add color and texture to your dream catchers.

6. Lace
Decorative trims, such as lace, can be used to create dream catcher webs or to hang as fringe in place of feathers.

7. Suede or leather cord
Use to create large frames, to hang completed dream catchers, or to wear small dream catchers as necklaces.

Note

When working with materials found in nature, such as branches, vines, and shells, it's important to note that the size, shape, and color of these items will vary. Despite following the instructions provided in this book, the appearance of your finished dream catchers will vary based on the materials you happen to find. As a result, you may need to make adjustments to the design to fit your actual materials.

Tools

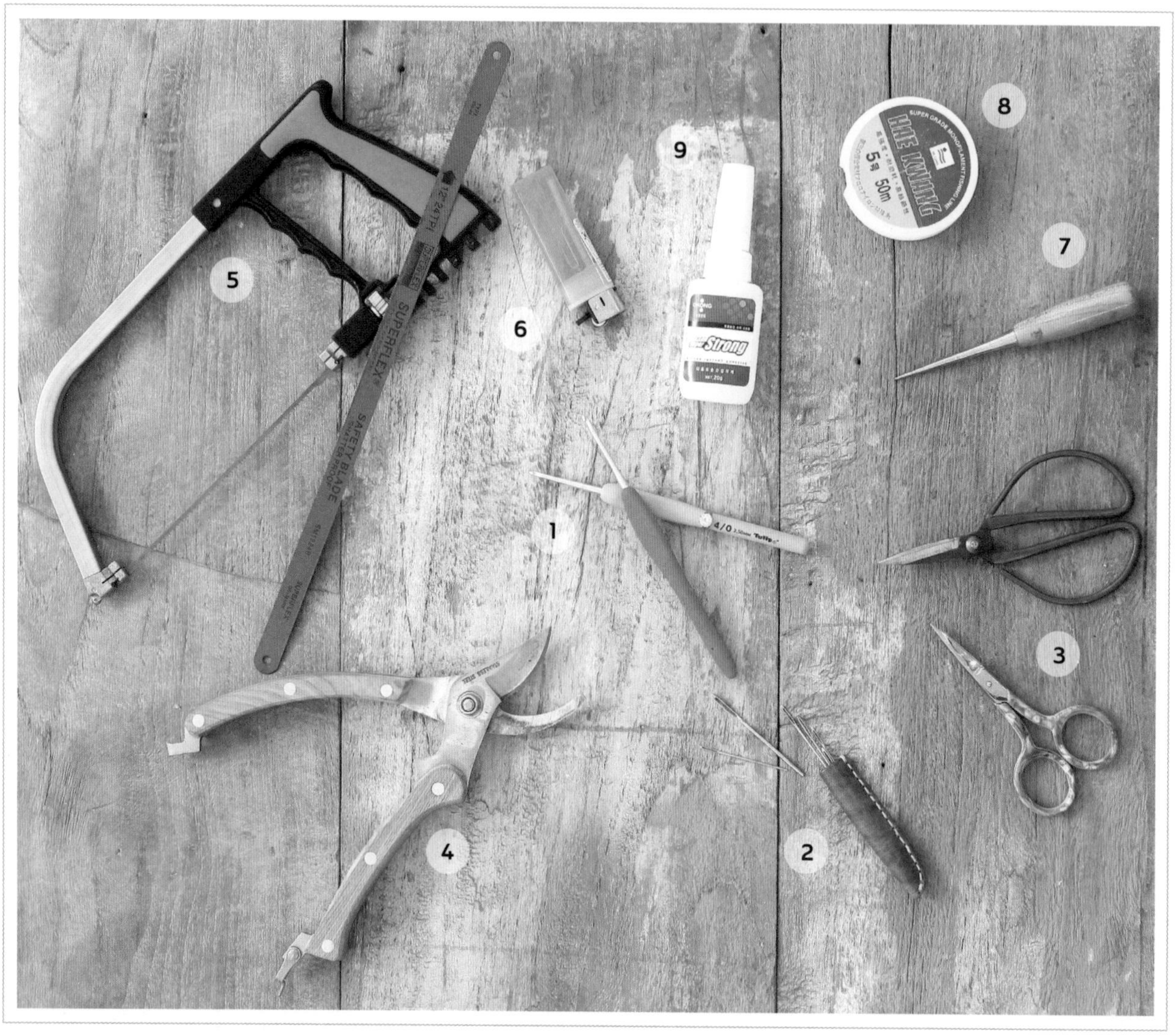

1. Crochet hooks

Size B and C hooks were used to create crocheted design elements, such as flowers and circle motifs, for certain projects.

2. Tapestry needles

Use to weave dream catcher webs, secure thread ends, and string beads.

3. Thread snips

Use to cut yarn, twine, and cord.

4. Pruning shears

You'll need these to cut and trim branches.

5. Hand saw

A small hand saw is useful to cut thick branches.

6. Lighter

Use a lighter to melt waxed twine ends for a neat and sturdy finish.

7. Awl

Use to enlarge the size of bead holes or to puncture holes in shells and branches.

8. Fishing line

For a nearly invisible finish, use clear fishing line to hang or secure components.

9. Glue

Use to attach decorative items, such as crochet motifs, feathers, or other embellishments.

THEME

1

Protection

"Happy Birthday my son!"

"Aren't you grateful you have me Mom?"

Leave it to my son to ask me if I'm grateful for him instead of just saying "thank you" when I wish him a happy birthday.

"Didn't I grow up to be such a strong, smart, and handsome guy?" he asks with his voice full of laughter.

I can't help laughing at his joke either. But he's right—I am thankful for him and am so proud of him for working so hard during his senior year of high school.

I wish all his dreams come true and he is happy as I secretly hang a miniature dream catcher on his backpack as he heads off to school.

Images opposite and above feature the Dream Catcher Bag Charm.
See page 20 for instructions.

Dream Catcher Bag Charm

Designed to hang on a bag, this good luck charm is made of willow and hawk feathers. Feathers are deeply revered in Native American culture and are believed to bring good energy.

Eagle and hawk feathers are especially valued as symbols of bravery, strength, and protection, so they are the perfect representation of a parent's desire to support and watch over their children.

Willow is known for its pain and fever reducing properties, so it is another good material for protecting a child's well-being.

Instructions on page 20

Dream Catcher Necklace

Let's use the same technique to create a miniature dream catcher necklace hanging from a long suede cord. In addition to being a good luck charm, it's also a fashionable accessory that goes well with a casual t-shirt or a sophisticated dress. When you're not wearing it, hang it on the rearview mirror of your car to encourage safe driving.

Instructions on page 21

DREAM CATCHER BAG CHARM

SHOWN ON PAGE 18

willow branch • hawk feather • waxed twine
assorted wooden beads • scissors • glue

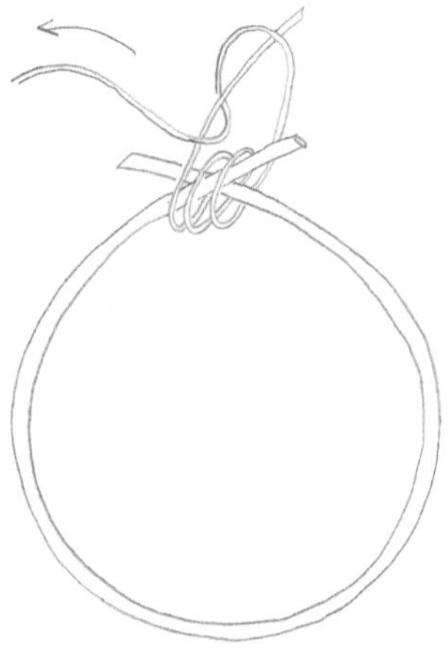

1 Bend the branch to make a circular frame about 2½ in (6 cm) in diameter. Tie the ends together with 1 yard (1 m) of waxed twine to tightly secure.

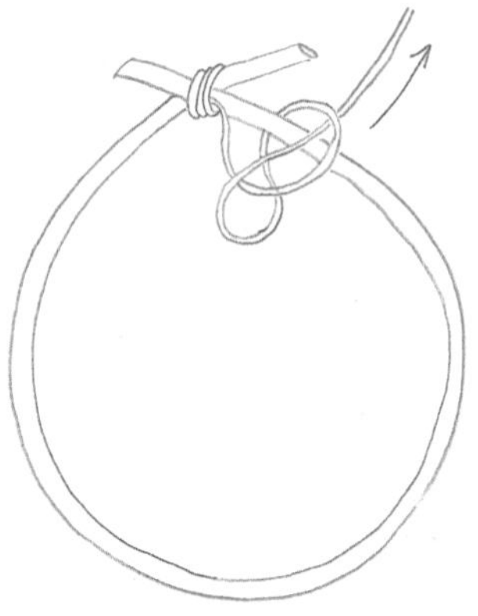

2 Holding the long end of the twine, tie it around the frame as shown above.

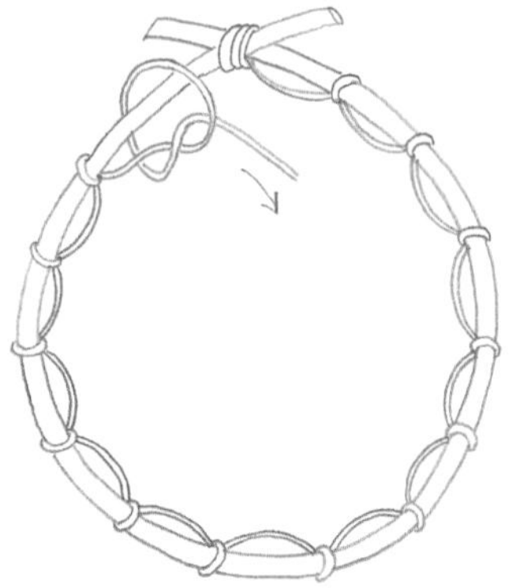

3 Continue tying the twine around the frame at equal intervals for a total of 15 loops.

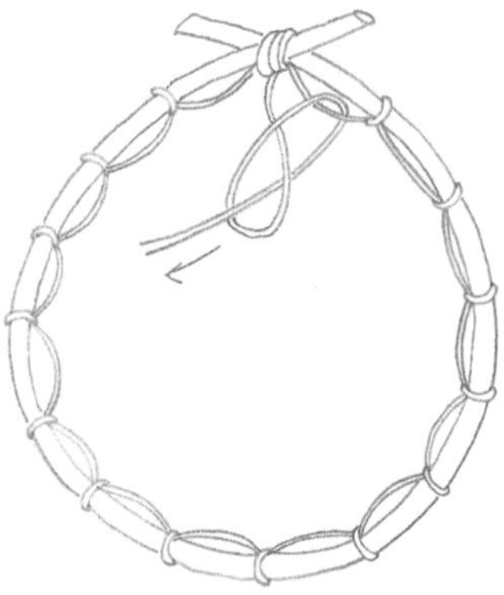

4 To make the second row of loops, make a knot at the center of each loop from the first row.

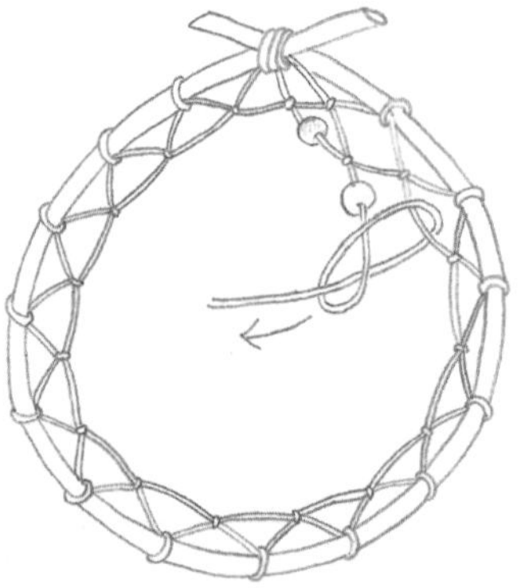

5 To make the third row, add a bead to each loop while tying the knots in the same way as step 4.

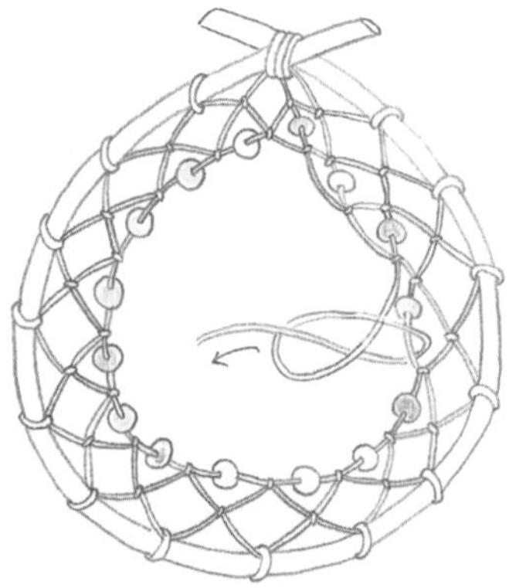

6 Follow the same process used in step 4 to make loops for rows four and five.

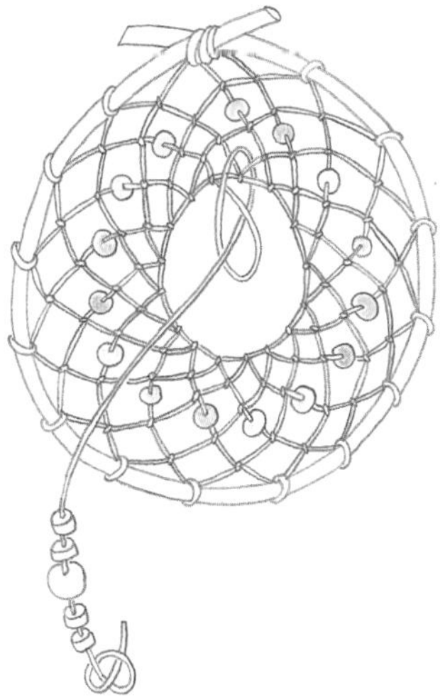

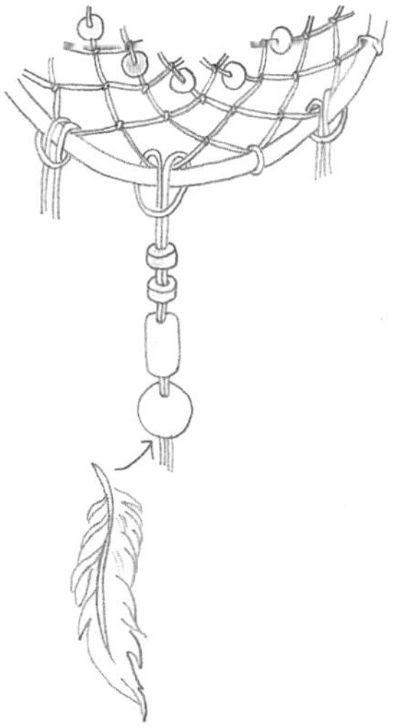

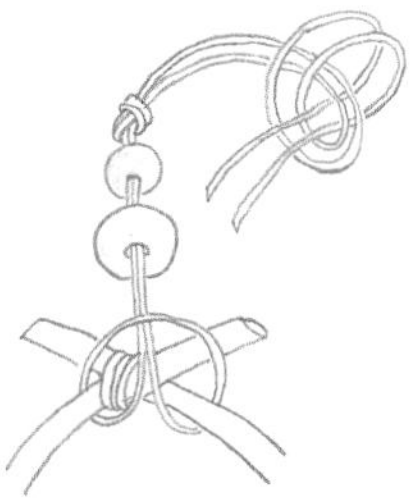

7 String five beads onto the remaining length of waxed twine. Tie a knot at the end of the twine to keep the beads in place.

8 Fold a 6 in (15 cm) piece of waxed twine in half and tie to the bottom of the frame as shown above. Thread four beads onto the piece of twine. Apply a dab of glue to a feather and insert into the hole of the final bead to secure in place. Repeat to add two more beaded strands.

9 Fold an 8 in (20 cm) piece of waxed twine in half and tie to the top of the frame. Thread a couple beads onto the piece of twine, then tie a knot to secure. Tie another knot at the end of the twine to create a hanging loop.

DREAM CATCHER NECKLACE

SHOWN ON PAGE 19

willow branch • small feathers with metal loops (purchased at a jewelry supply store)
waxed twine • suede cord • assorted wooden beads • scissors • glue

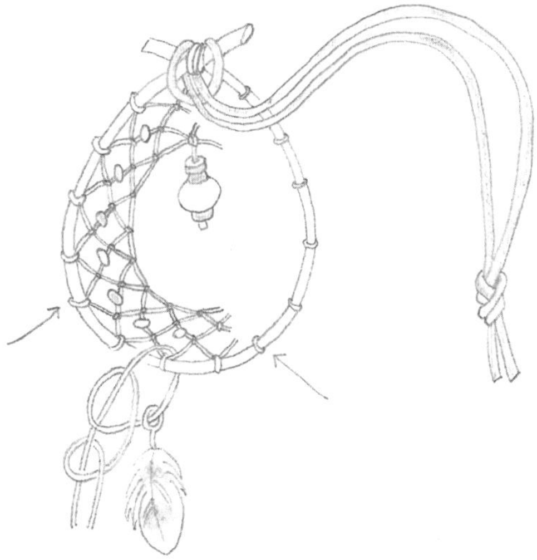

1. Select a branch that is thin and flexible. Bend the branch to make an oval frame about 1½ in (4 cm) in diameter. Tie the ends together with 1 yard (1 m) of waxed twine.
2. Follow the same process used in steps 2–7 for the Dream Catcher Bag Charm, reducing the number of loops or rows if necessary.
3. Fold a long piece of suede cord in half and tie to the top of the frame. Tie the ends of the suede cord together to create a loop.
4. Use waxed twine to tie the feathers to the bottom of the frame at the positions indicated by the arrows.

THEME

2

Beauty

The only flowers that I've seen for the past several months are those that bloom from my crochet hook and bring the dry branches of my dream catchers to life.

But today, a warm breeze drifts through my open window as winter yields to spring. For some time now, I've been keeping my eye out for the azaleas that bloom in the mountains at the beginning of the season.

Once the azaleas fall, pure white magnolias and light pink cherry blossoms burst to life. After the cherry blossom petals are scattered by the spring rain, wild roses bloom in May.

The roses give way to summer lilies, blue hydrangeas, delicate cosmos, and China asters. It's as if the flowers are running a relay race and passing the baton from one beautiful plant to the next.

Flower Bouquet Dream Catcher

This crochet flower dream catcher was inspired by my garden. Spiral-shaped petals and verdant green leaves appear to bloom from the very center of the dream catcher's web. I used a coordinating color scheme for the flowers, but feel free to experiment with the color, size, and arrangement to create your own unique look.

Instructions on page 28

Flower Vine Dream Catcher

Tie a horizontal branch across the bottom of the circular frame, then add crocheted flowers and leaves to make it appear as if a vine is climbing along the dream catcher. A single feather complements the simple vertical woven lines of this design without stealing attention from the beautiful flowers.

Instructions on page 30

FLOWER BOUQUET DREAM CATCHER

SHOWN ON PAGE 24

vine • *feathers* • *waxed twine* • *assorted shades of green, pink, and white yarn*
crochet needle • *tapestry needle* • *assorted wooden beads* • *scissors* • *glue*

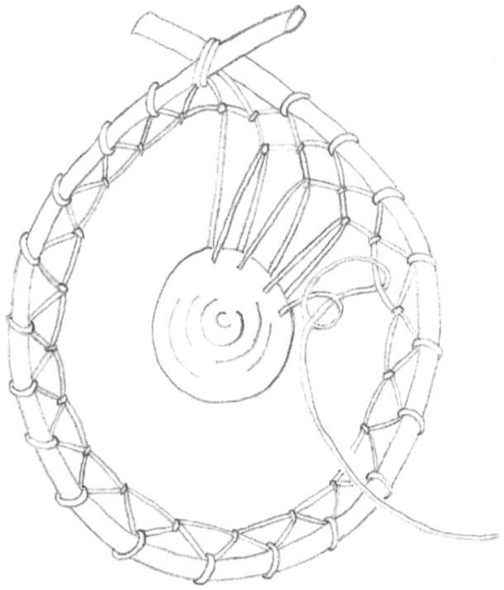

1 Bend the vine to make a circular frame about 8 in (20 cm) in diameter and secure with waxed twine. Next, tie the twine around the frame at equal intervals to make a total of 20 loops, then weave two more rows (refer to steps 3 and 4 on page 20). Do not cut the twine. Use white yarn to crochet a circular motif (refer to step 3 on page 102 for crochet chart). This will serve as a foundation for the crocheted flowers and leaves. Use a tapestry needle and twine to attach the circular motif to the center of the dream catcher as shown at left.

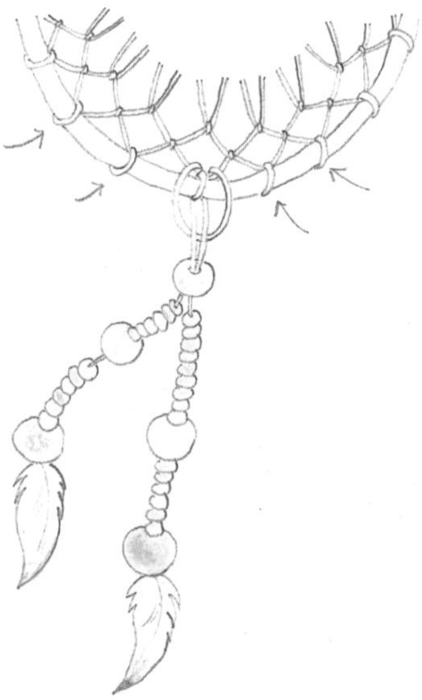

2 Cut five pieces of waxed twine. Fold each piece in half and tie to the bottom of the frame at the positions indicated by the arrows. String beads and glue feathers onto each strand as shown at left.

A × 1

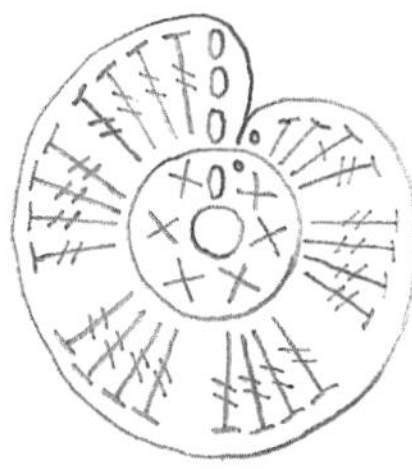

B × 2

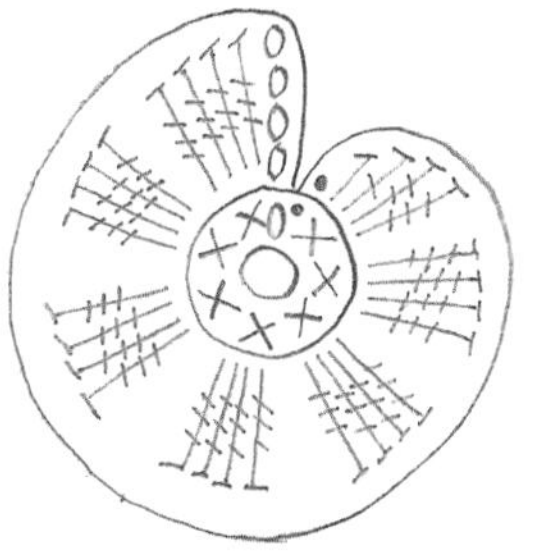

C × 1

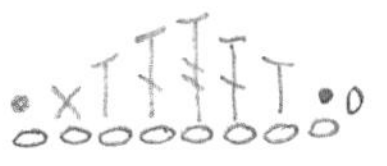

D × 2

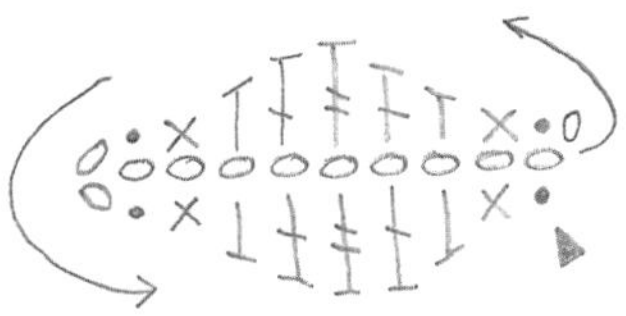

E × 4

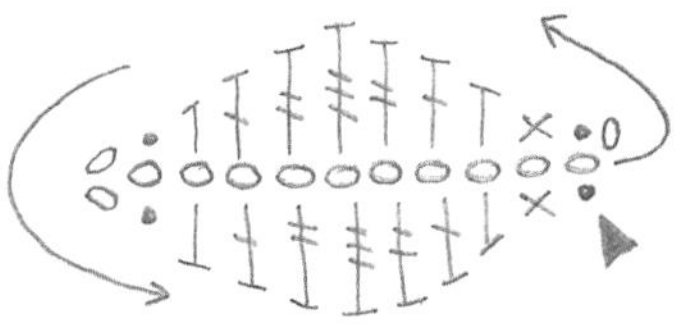

F × 4

3 Crochet the flowers and leaves following the charts shown above. Use green yarn for all flower centers (A-C), white yarn for A, white and dark pink yarn for B, and light pink yarn for C. Make a total of 10 leaves using various shades of green yarn.

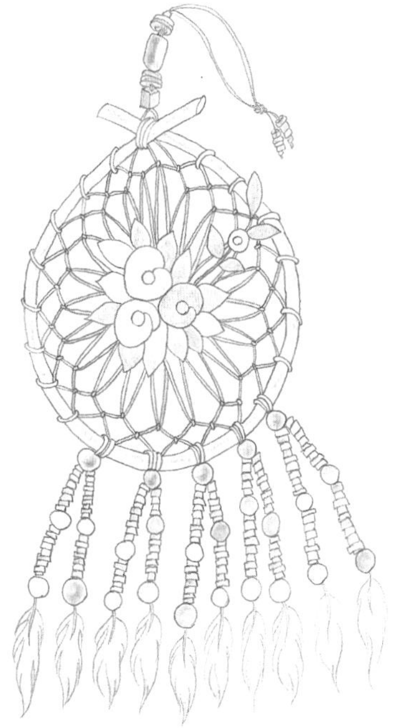

4 Crochet G (refer to step 5 on page 31 for crochet chart). Arrange the crocheted flowers and leaves at the center of the dream catcher. Glue or sew to the circular motif from step 1. Tie a hanging loop at the top of the dream catcher and add beads as desired.

FLOWER VINE DREAM CATCHER

SHOWN ON PAGE 26

vines • ostrich feather • waxed twine • assorted shades of green, pink, and white yarn crochet needle • tapestry needle • assorted wooden beads red and white beads • scissors • glue

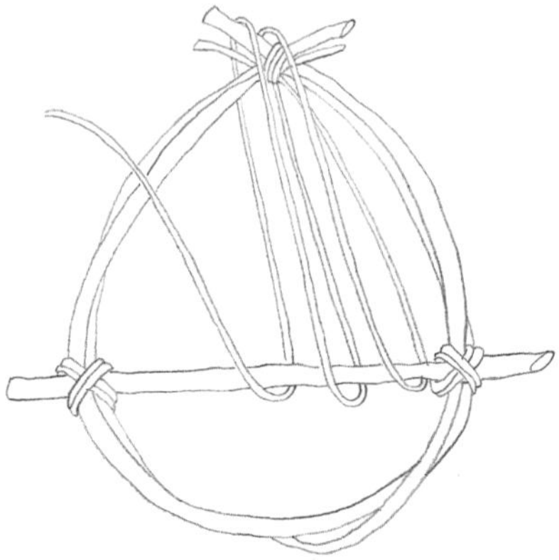

1 Bend the vines to make a vertical oval frame about 8 in (20 cm) in diameter and secure with waxed twine. Do not cut the twine—leave a long tail that measures a few yards long. Align a straight branch along the bottom third of the frame and secure in place using pieces of waxed twine.

2 Wrap the waxed twine left long in step 1 around the horizontal branch, then around the top of the frame. Repeat several times to form a triangle across the center of the frame. Make sure the pull the twine taut as you wrap.

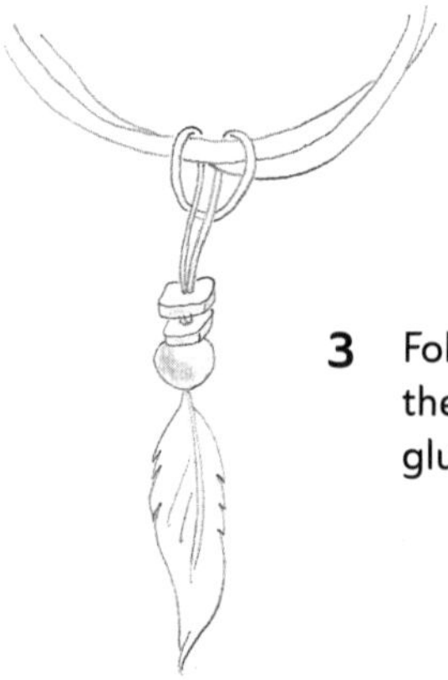

3 Fold a piece of waxed twine in half and tie to the bottom of the frame. String beads and glue the feather in place as shown at left.

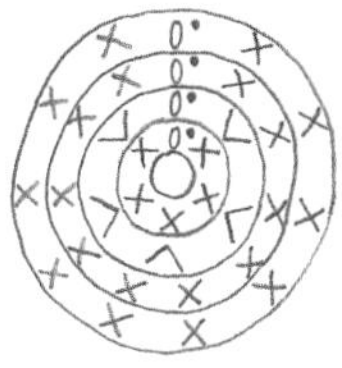

A × 1

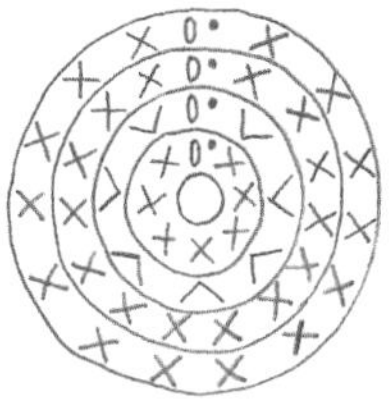

B × 2

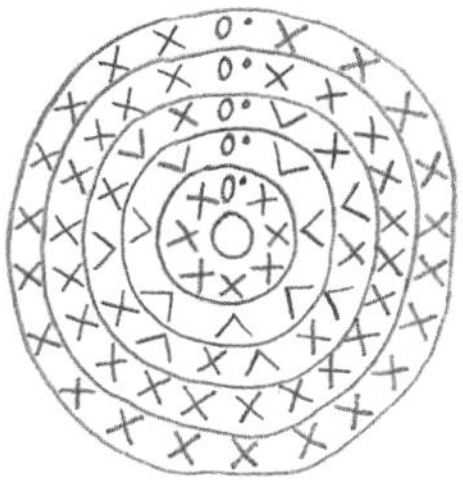

C × 1

4 Crochet the flowers following the charts shown above. Use dark pink yarn for A, pink and dark pink yarn for B, and light pink yarn for C.

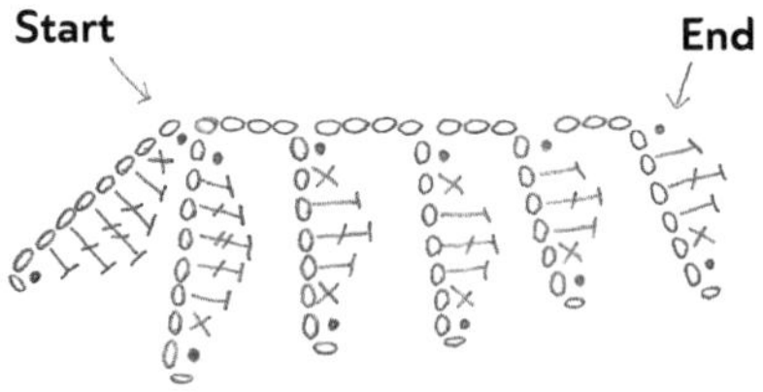

G × 1

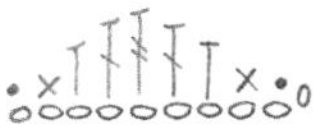

D × 3

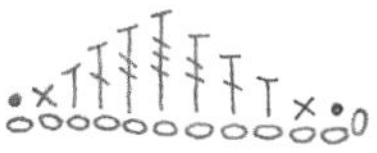

E × 3

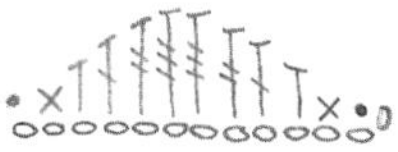

F × 2

5 Crochet the leaves following the charts shown above. Use various shades of green yarn.

6 Glue the leaves and flowers to the horizontal branch and vertical web, following the layout shown above. Sew the red and white beads to the center of the flowers. Tie a hanging loop at the top of the dream catcher and add beads as desired.

THEME

3

Individuality

Even if I know that another route is faster and more direct, I always prefer to take the unfamiliar path. When I was required to wear a school uniform as a child, I would change the buttons on my blouse, just so I wouldn't be dressed the same as everyone else.

I grow tired of routine and crave the excitement that comes along with trying new things. I like to think that this keeps me young!

Images opposite and above feature the Triangle Dream Catcher.
See page 38 for instructions.

Triangle Dream Catcher

Most dream catchers feature a circular frame filled with a woven web and embellished with feathers. For a modern, minimalist approach, try a triangular frame with elegant tassel fringe.

Instructions on page 38

Vertical Net Dream Catcher

This simple dream catcher features a triangular vertical web and fringe made from wooden beads. The earthy colors and textures of the beads give this design a calm, natural feel. As an added bonus, the wooden beads make playful, rhythmical sounds when the dream catcher drifts in the breeze.

Instructions on page 39

TRIANGLE DREAM CATCHER

SHOWN ON PAGE 34

branches • assorted gemstone beads • waxed twine • circular wooden beads
white tassel trim • scissors

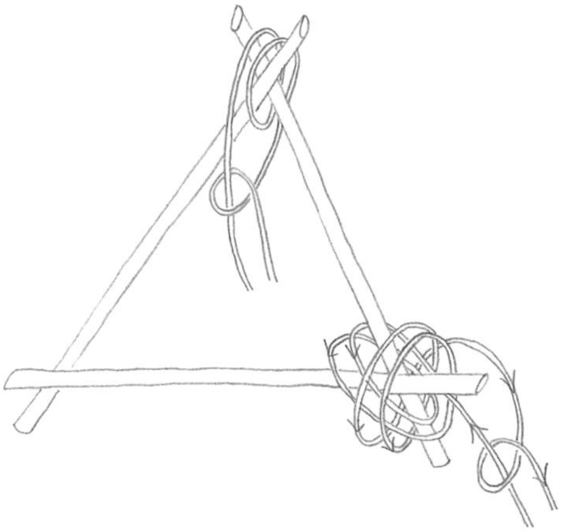

1 Use waxed twine to tie three 8 in (20 cm) straight branches together in a triangle. Do not cut the twine at the top of the frame—leave a long tail that measures a few yards long.

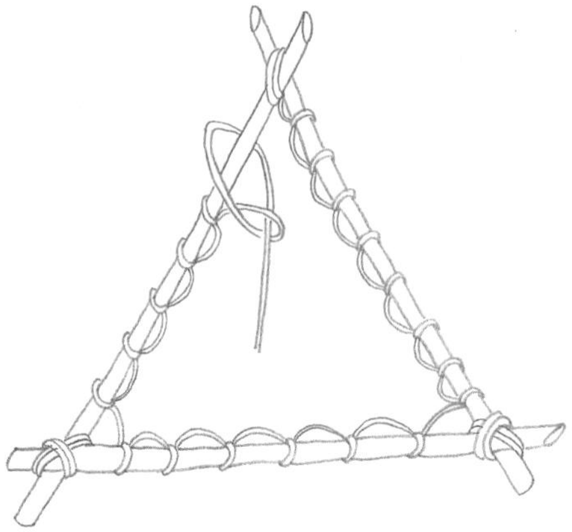

2 Tie the twine left long in step 1 around the frame at equal intervals to make a total of 20–22 loops.

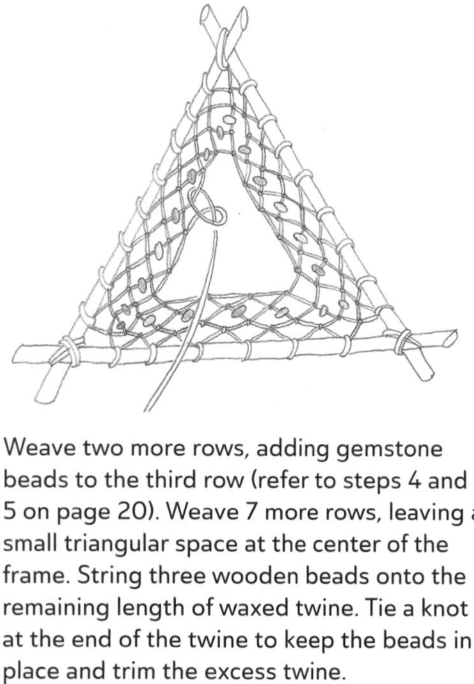

3 Weave two more rows, adding gemstone beads to the third row (refer to steps 4 and 5 on page 20). Weave 7 more rows, leaving a small triangular space at the center of the frame. String three wooden beads onto the remaining length of waxed twine. Tie a knot at the end of the twine to keep the beads in place and trim the excess twine.

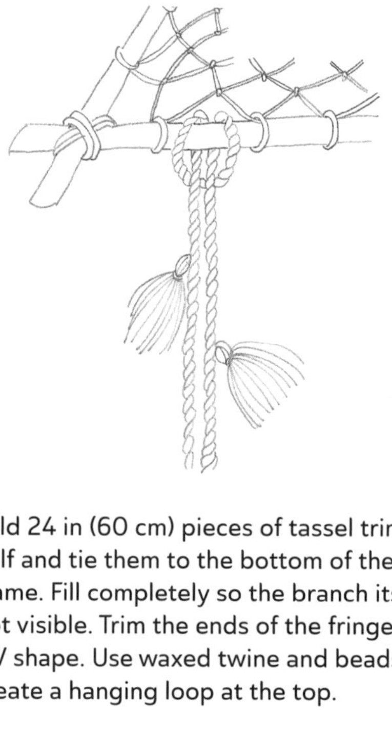

4 Fold 24 in (60 cm) pieces of tassel trim in half and tie them to the bottom of the frame. Fill completely so the branch itself is not visible. Trim the ends of the fringe into a V shape. Use waxed twine and beads to create a hanging loop at the top.

VERTICAL NET DREAM CATCHER

SHOWN ON PAGE 36

branch • assorted wooden beads and rings • waxed twine • scissors

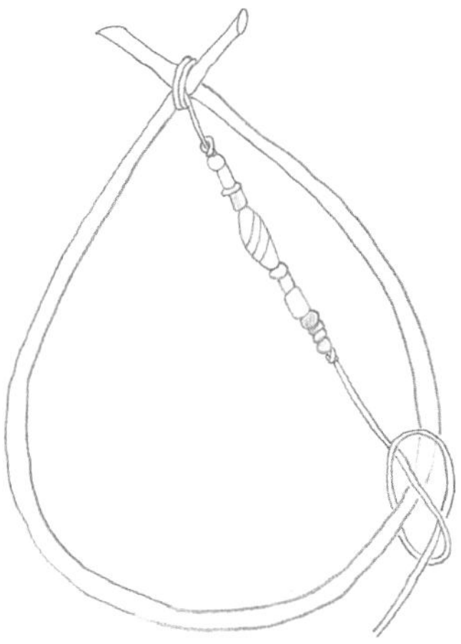

1 Bend the branch to make a vertical oval frame about 8 in (20 cm) in diameter and secure with waxed twine. String beads onto the twine, then tie to the bottom of the frame. Make sure to tie knots at the beginning and end when stringing the beads so they stay positioned at the center of the frame.

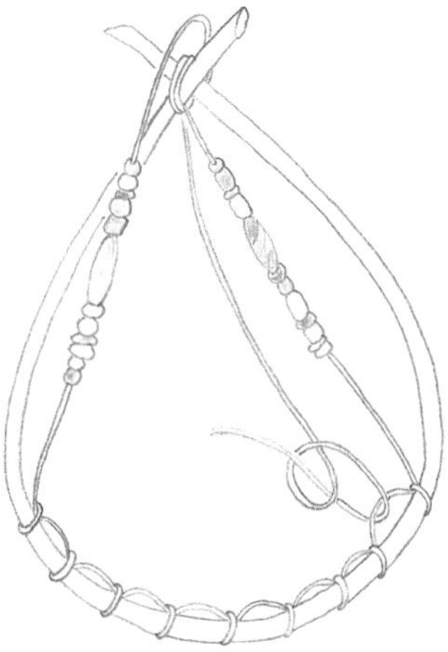

2 Tie the twine around the bottom of the frame at equal intervals to make eight loops. String beads onto the twine, pull taut, and wrap it around the top of the frame. Bring the twine back down to the bottom of the frame and tie a knot at the center of the first loop on the right.

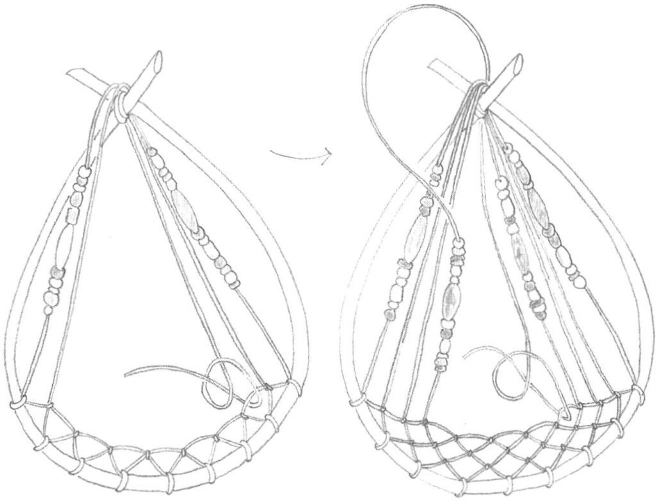

3 Use this process to weave the triangular vertical web. Leave two plain strands in between each beaded strand for balance.

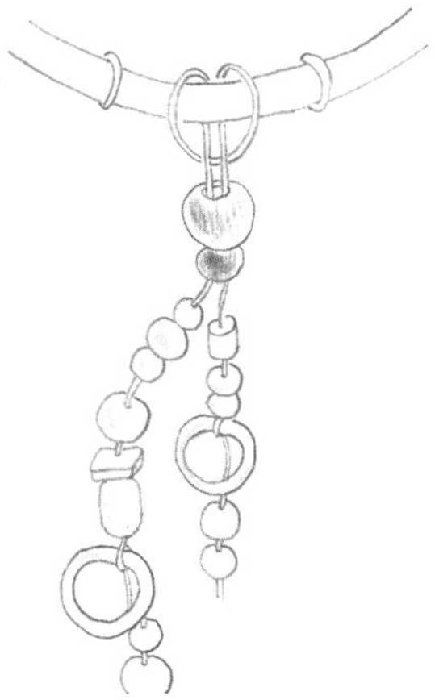

4 Once the triangular vertical web is complete, cut five 16 in (40 cm) pieces of waxed twine, fold in half, and tie to the bottom of the frame. String assorted wooden beads and rings onto the twine and secure with knots. Use waxed twine and beads to create a hanging loop at the top.

THEME

4

Good Fortune

I had been longing to visit the sea, but once I arrived, I spent more time sorting through the piles of sea glass and shells in the sand than gazing at the blue horizon.

Seashells, round pebbles, driftwood—these natural materials are more precious to me than expensive jewels. I love hunting for "mermaids' tears"—pieces of broken glass that have been weathered by the waves, wind, and sand and transformed into smooth gems of beautiful, subdued color.

Sea Glass Dream Catcher

Crafted from sea glass, driftwood, and shells, this dream catcher makes for a refreshing summer decoration, especially when hung in a window where the transparent glass can catch the sunlight.

Instructions on page 46

Summer Dream Catcher

Commemorate a vacation or day spent at the beach with this unique dream catcher. Connect driftwood, shells, sea glass, and feathers to form an artful wall hanging, then add a small dream catcher pendant.

Instructions on page 47

SEA GLASS DREAM CATCHER

SHOWN ON PAGE 42

branches • waxed twine • sea glass • driftwood • seashells, starfish or other items collected from the beach gemstone beads • assorted wooded beads • clear fishing line • scissors • glue • an awl or drill

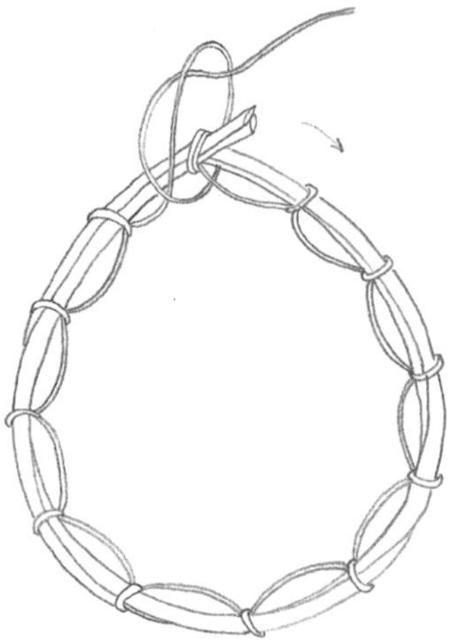

1 Bend the branch to make a circular frame about 8 in (20 cm) in diameter and secure with waxed twine. Use the waxed twine to tie 12 loops to the frame.

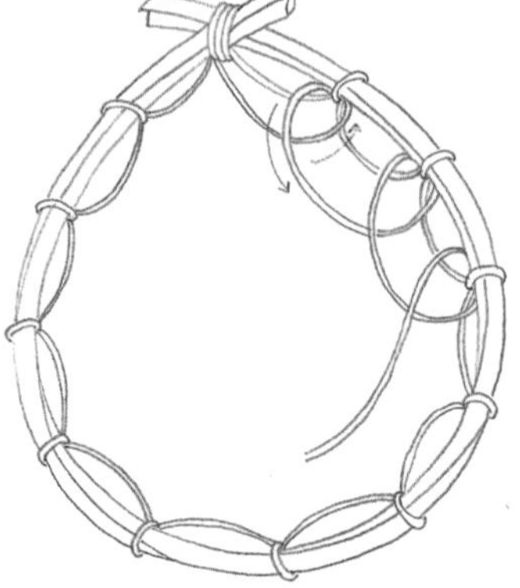

2 Make a second row by looping the waxed twine as shown by the arrows above.

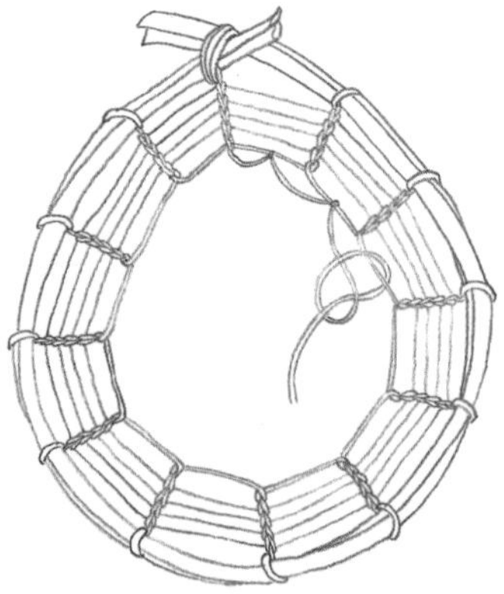

3 Follow the process shown in step 2 to make a total of five rows. To make the sixth row, make a knot at the center of each loop from the fifth row.

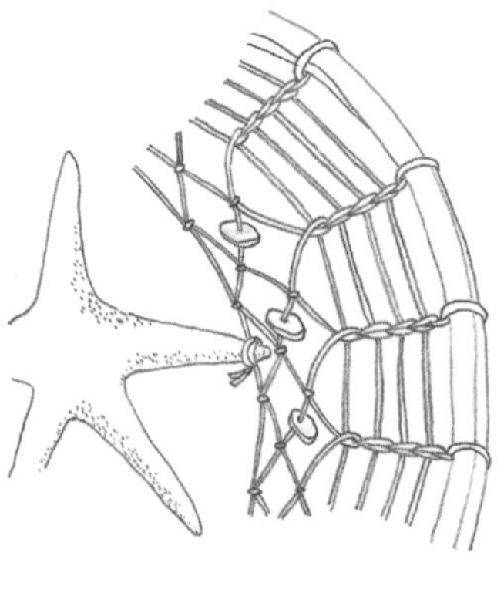

4 To make the seventh row, add a gemstone bead to each loop while tying the knots in the same way as step 3. Follow the process shown in step 3 to make two more rows. Next, position a starfish at the center of the web and secure in place using clear fishing line.

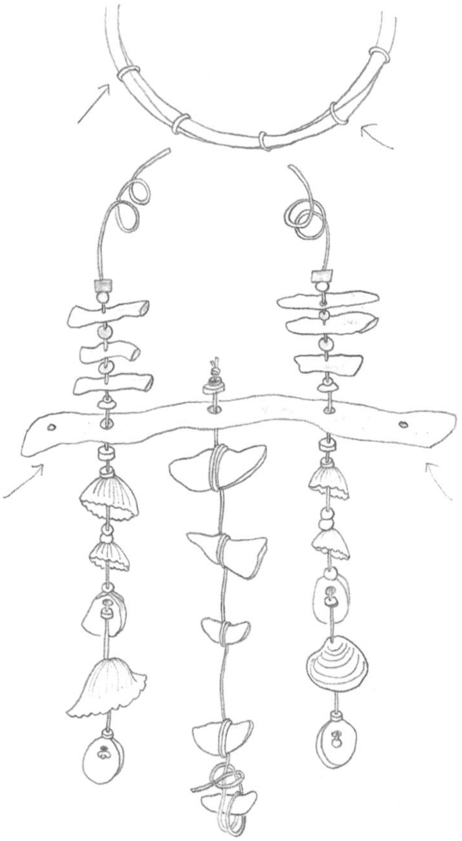

5 Make five holes in a large piece of driftwood. Insert a long piece of waxed twine through the second hole in from each end and string with seashells, beads, and small pieces of driftwood, using knots to secure. Tie these pieces of waxed twine to the bottom of the frame at the positions indicated by the arrows. Insert shorter pieces of waxed twine through the three remaining holes and string with sea glass. Use waxed twine and beads to create a hanging loop at the top.

SUMMER DREAM CATCHER

SHOWN ON PAGE 44

branch • waxed twine • sea glass • driftwood • seashells or other items collected from the beach assorted wooden beads • feathers • scissors • glue • an awl or drill

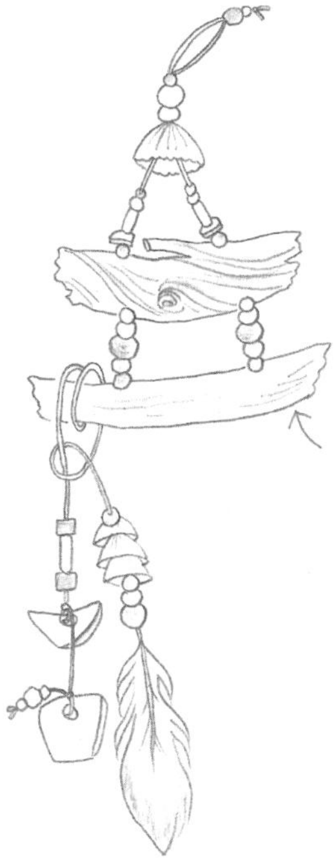

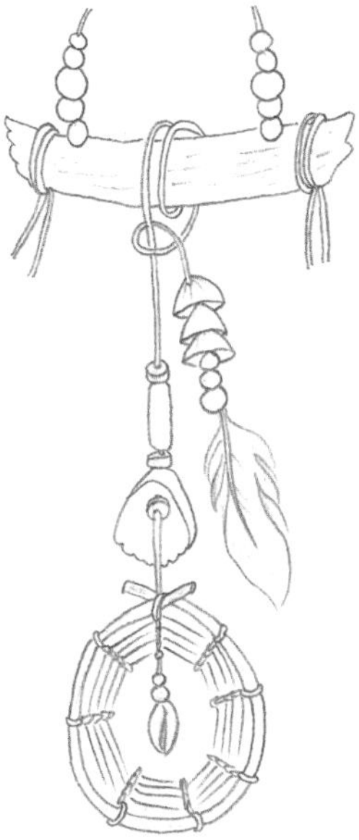

1 Use an awl or drill to make holes at each end of the pieces of driftwood. Note: The pieces of driftwood used here were approximately 8 in (20 cm) long. Insert a piece of waxed twine through the holes in the driftwood and string with beads and seashells, making a hanging loop at the top and connecting the two pieces of driftwood as shown above. Tie two pieces of waxed twine to the bottom piece of driftwood and string with beads, sea glass, seashells, and feathers.

2 Follow the same process used in steps 1–3 on page 46 to weave a small dream catcher pendant. After weaving five rows, string an assortment of seashells onto the remaining waxed twine so they hang at the center of the web. String the dream catcher pendant, beads, seashells, and feathers onto a piece of waxed twine and tie to the center of the bottom piece of driftwood.

THEME

5

Grace

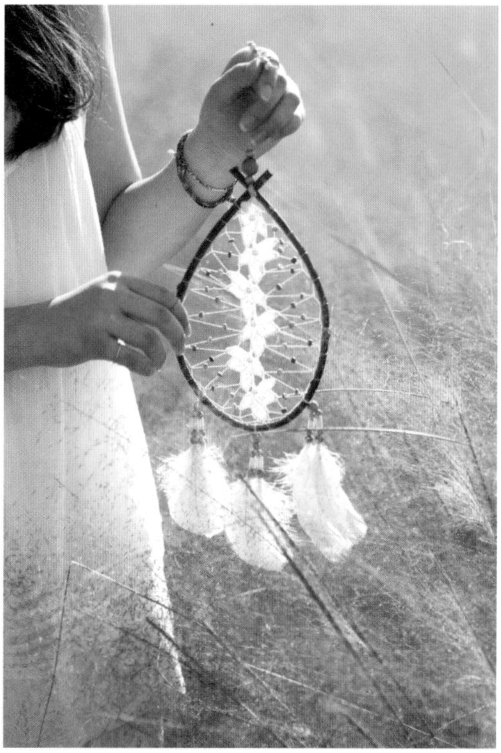

My teenage daughter loves dressing up in pretty dresses and sparkly blouses, while I was always more comfortable wearing a loose t-shirt and jeans at her age. Sometimes, I think that she was meant to be born as an elegant lady of history who dressed in the finest lace.

Images opposite and above feature the Lace Dream Catcher.
See page 52 for instructions.

Lace Dream Catcher

Use a strip of store-bought lace to form the foundation of the dream catcher's web and create an artsy, feminine design. Colorful beads and feathers complement the beautiful white lace and make this dream catcher a lovely gift for a girlfriend's birthday or bridal shower.

Instructions on page 52

Miniature Flower Dream Catcher

Fussy cut a flower from a piece of lace and attach it to the center of a dream catcher's web, then layer a crocheted flower on top for even more texture and dimension. A luxurious white ostrich feather adds a touch of elegance and grace.

Instructions on page 53

LACE DREAM CATCHER

SHOWN ON PAGE 50

branch • waxed twine • assorted wooden beads • floral lace
feathers • scissors • glue • tapestry needle

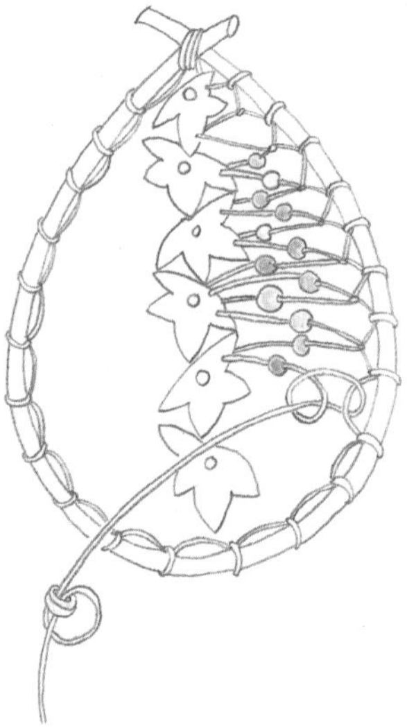

1 Bend the branch to make a vertical oval frame and secure with waxed twine. Use the waxed twine to tie 24 loops to the frame (refer to step 3 on page 20). Cut a piece of lace the same length as the frame and position it at the center. Use a tapestry needle to sew the waxed twine to the lace, then tie it to the loops, adding wooden beads as you work.

2 Fold three pieces of waxed twine in half and tie to the bottom of the frame at the positions indicated by the arrows. String beads and feathers onto the twine as shown above. Use waxed twine and beads to create a hanging loop at the top.

MINIATURE FLOWER DREAM CATCHER

SHOWN ON PAGE 51

branch • waxed twine • assorted wooden beads • floral lace • white ostrich feather
light pink yarn • crochet hook • scissors • glue • tapestry needle

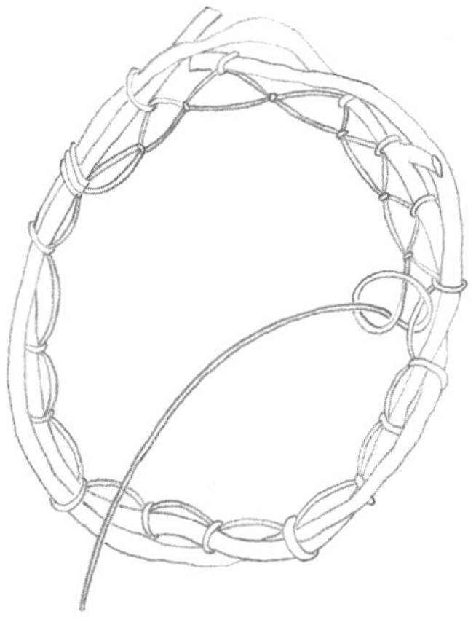

1 Bend the branch to make a circular frame about 2¾ in (7 cm) in diameter and secure with waxed twine. Use waxed twine to tie 16 loops to the frame, then weave another row (refer to steps 3 and 4 on page 20).

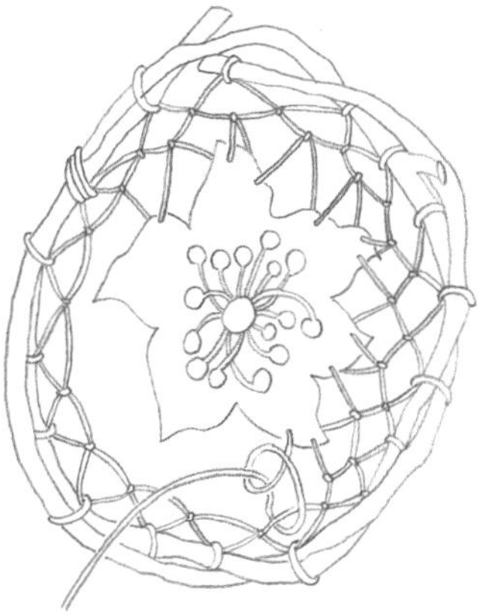

2 Fussy cut a flower from the lace and position it at the center of the frame. Use a tapestry needle to sew the waxed twine to the lace, then tie it to the loops of the second row.

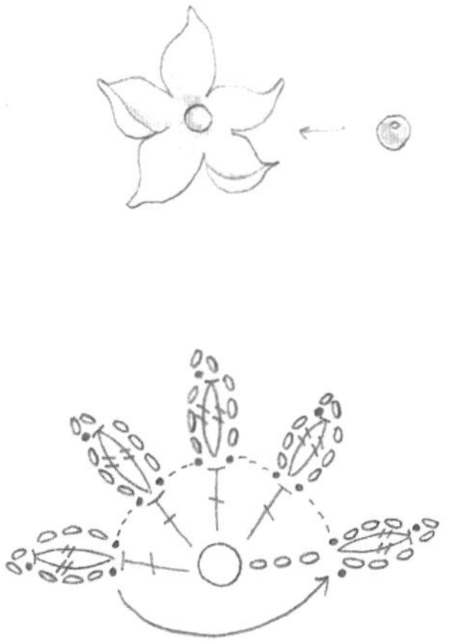

3 Crochet a light pink flower following the chart shown above. Sew a pink bead to the center of the flower. Sew the crocheted flower to the center of the lace flower.

4 Fold a 4 in (10 cm) piece of waxed twine in half and tie it to the bottom of the frame. String beads onto the twine, then glue the ostrich feather inside the hole of the final bead. Use waxed twine and beads to create a hanging loop at the top.

THEME

6

Patience

Despite enduring traffic jams to get to the campsite, sleeping on the hard ground, and the lack of running water, spending time in nature refreshes the mind and soul. The benefits of quality time spent gathered around the campfire, breathing clean air and sleeping under the stars, far outweigh the lack of modern conveniences. These colorful dream catchers celebrate the romance and spirit of nature.

Image features the Dream Catcher Garland.
See page 61 for instructions

Camping Dream Catcher

This festive dream catcher will add a bit of color and cheer to your campsite. Hang it outside your tent to invite pleasant dreams and comfortable slumber. The vertical orientation of the pendants is perfect for hanging from a tree limb.

Instructions on page 60

Dream Catcher Garland

This design uses the same techniques as the Camping Dream Catcher on page 56, but the pendants are connected horizontally to form a garland that can be hung across the entrance of a tent. Colorful fabric tassels add a festive touch.

Instructions on page 61

CAMPING DREAM CATCHER

SHOWN ON PAGE 56

branches • assorted colors of yarn • white cotton yarn • round wooden beads
striped ribbon • scissors • tapestry needle

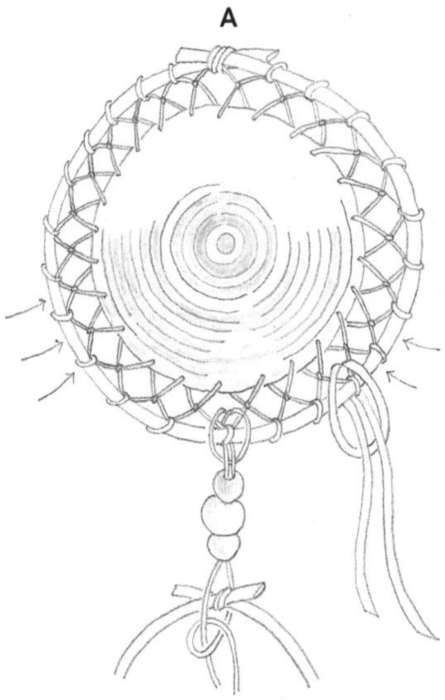

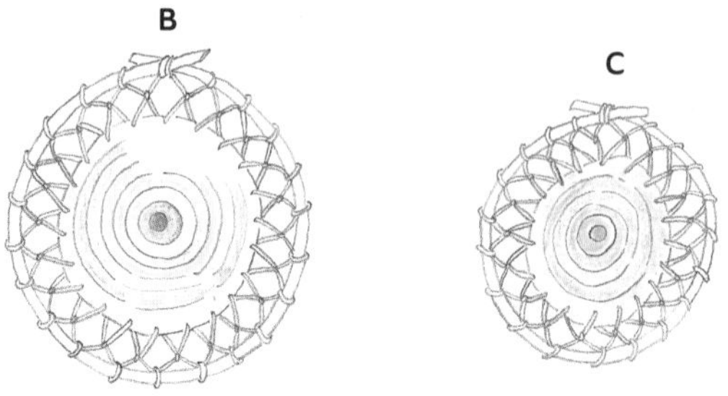

1 Bend the branches to make three circular frames: 8 in (20 cm) in diameter for A, 4¾ in (12 cm) in diameter for B, and 2¾ in (7 cm) in diameter for C. Crochet the circular motifs using a different color of yarn for each round. Refer to step 3 on page 102 for the crochet chart, but use 13 rounds for A, 8 rounds for B, and 6 rounds for C.

2 Refer to step 3 on page 20 for instructions on tying the white cotton yarn to the frames (adjust the number of loops accordingly). Use a tapestry needle to sew the crochet motifs to their corresponding frames.

3 Use white cotton yarn strung with round wooden beads to tie them together vertically in the following order: A, B, C.

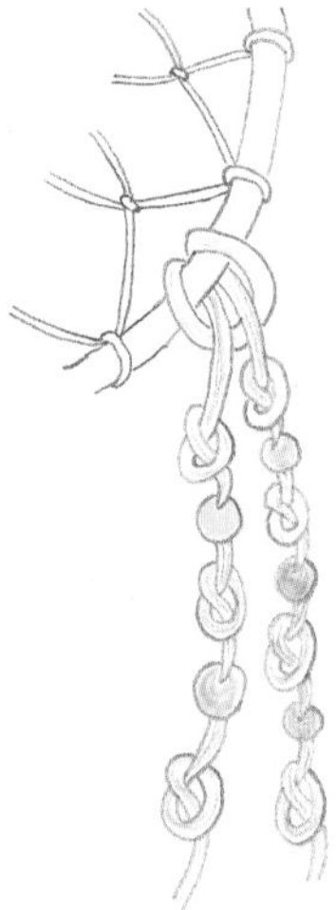

4 Fold pieces of ribbon in half and tie to the bottom of each frame. Use six pieces of ribbon for A, four pieces of ribbon for B, and three pieces of ribbon for C. String beads onto the ribbon, tying knots between each bead to secure in place. Use ribbon and beads to create a hanging loop at the top.

DREAM CATCHER GARLAND

SHOWN ON PAGE 58

branches • assorted colors of yarn • white cotton yarn • round wooden beads striped ribbon • suede cord • scissors • tapestry needle

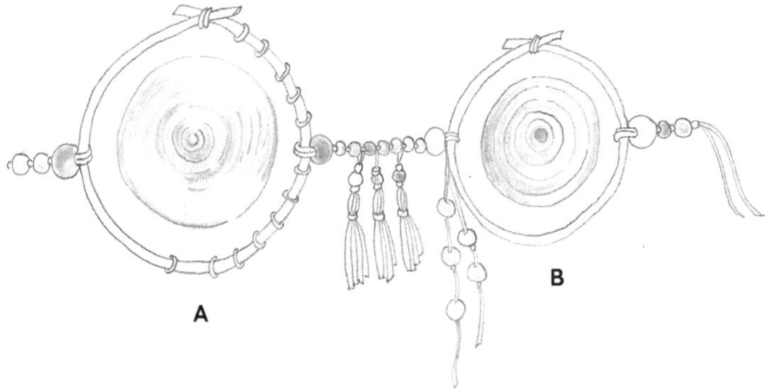

1 Follow steps 1 and 2 on page 60 to make A-C. Arrange the pendants horizontally in the following order: C, A, B. Connect the pendants using pieces of suede cord strung with wooden beads.

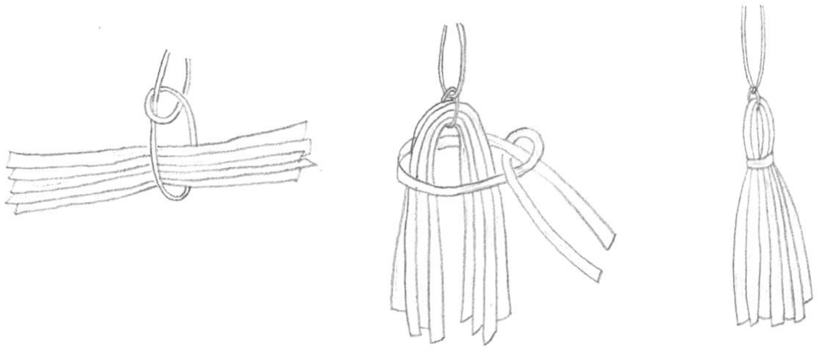

2 Cut several 8 in (20 cm) pieces of ribbon. Arrange the pieces of ribbon in a horizontal bundle and tie together at the center. Fold the pieces down and tie the bundle together near the top. Repeat to make five more tassels.

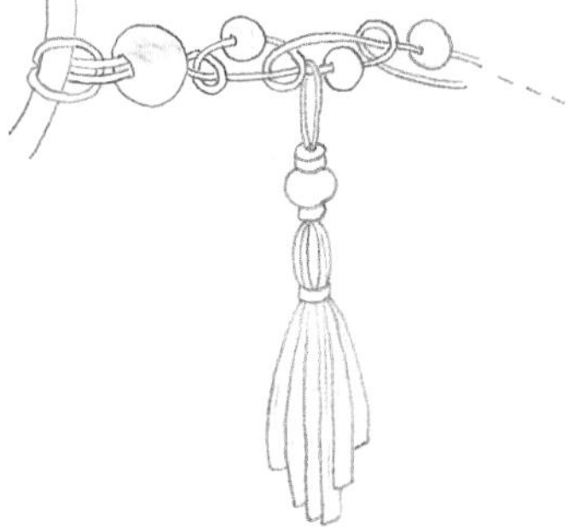

3 String beads onto each tassel, then tie three tassels to the suede cord between pendants C and A and three tassels to the suede cord between pendants A and B.

4 Use suede cord and beads to create a hanging loop at each end.

THEME

7

Prayers

"Young-Ran, how are you doing?"

My aunt, who is a nun, calls me to say hello one day.

Living the life of a busy wife and mother for the last 20 years, it causes me to choke up when I hear her call me by my given name using such a tender voice.

"I always pray for you."

Hearing these words, the tears start flowing in earnest now. The fact that someone is praying for me without asking for anything in return— what could be more touching and comforting than that?

Suddenly, I feel my wobbly legs grow stronger and feel the heavy burdens lifted from my shoulders.

"Auntie, I am happy and healthy, thanks to your prayers."

Images opposite and above feature God's Eye. *See page 66 for instructions.*

God's Eye

Over the years, God's Eyes have become a popular craft at summer camps and schools and are universally known as good luck charms. Since every strand of yarn is woven with hope, they make excellent gifts for someone in need of prayer or for a friend or neighbor moving into a new house.

Instructions on page 66

The History of the God's Eye: The Dream Catcher's Cousin

God's Eyes originated with the Huichol, the indigenous people of present day western Mexico. They are composed of two sticks tied together in a cross formation, then wound with yarn to create a diamond-shaped pattern. The four points of the cross represent the four elements—fire, earth, air, and water—while the center was believed to serve as a portal between the spirit world and the mortal world. The gods could look the through the eye to watch over the humans and the humans could use the eye to ask for help from the gods.

GOD'S EYE

SHOWN ON PAGE 64

branches • assorted colors of yarn • waxed twine • circular wooden beads
oval wooden beads • feathers • scissors • glue

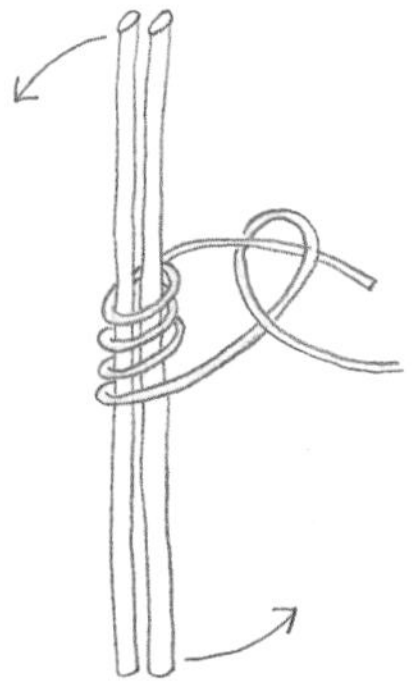

1 Align two 8 in (20 cm) long straight branches. Use a piece of yarn to tie them together at the center.

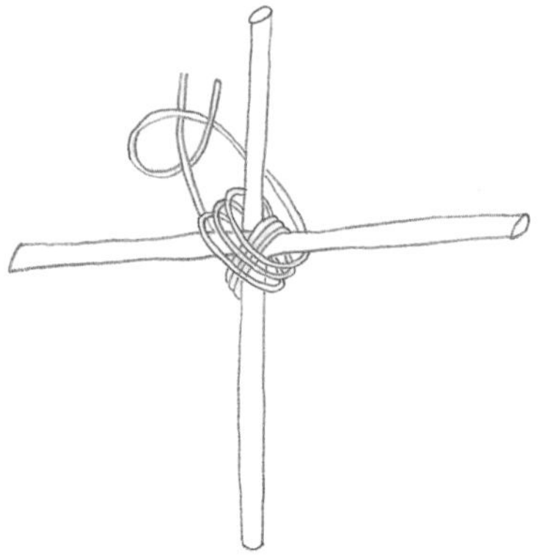

2 Rotate one of the branches 90 degrees to form a cross shape. Wind the yarn around the branches diagonally and tie a knot to hold the cross shape in place.

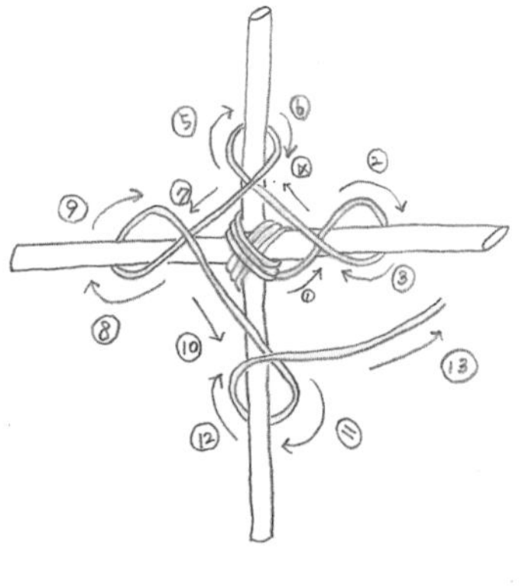

3 Using another color of yarn, wrap the yarn around the cross following the numerical order shown above. Pull tightly as you wrap to create a neatly woven diamond shape.

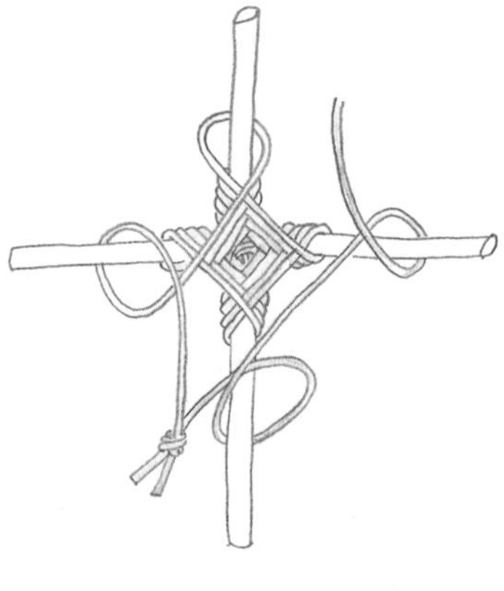

4 Use the same process to weave several rounds of diamonds. When you're ready to change colors, tie the new piece of yarn to the end of the old one, then continue wrapping.

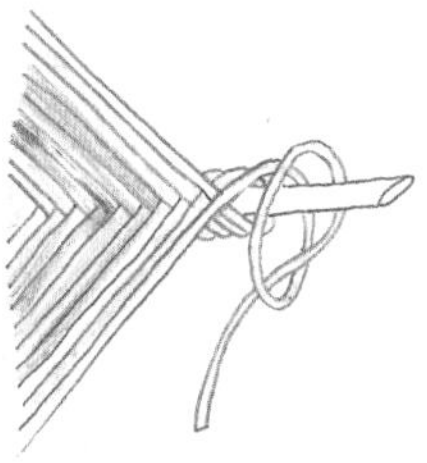

5 Stop weaving when there is about 3/4 in (2 cm) of space left at the end of each branch. Secure the yarn by tying a knot.

6 Bend another branch to make a circular frame. Align the God's eye on top of the circular frame and tie in place using waxed twine.

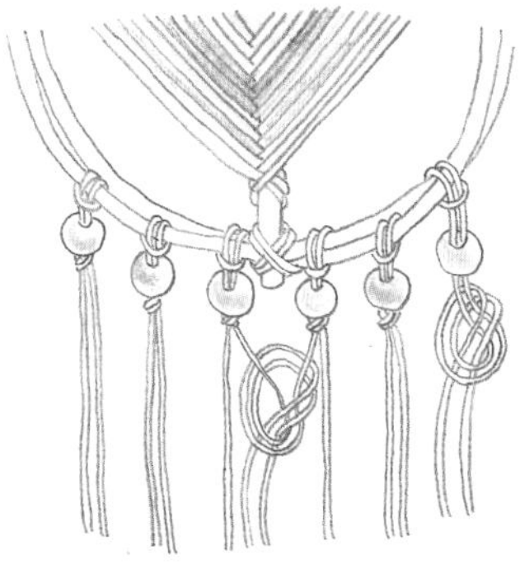

7 Cut six 24 in (60 cm) pieces of waxed twine, fold in half, and tie to the bottom of the circular frame. Thread a circular wooden bead onto each piece and tie a knot. Next, bring adjacent strands together and knot. Continue threading beads onto the pieces of waxed twine and knotting to create a net, as shown in step 8.

8 Thread oval wooden beads onto the end of each piece, knot, then glue a feather inside the hole of each oval wooden bead.

God’s Eye Wall Hanging

God's eyes may be made with just a couple tree branches and some scraps of yarn, yet they transform into striking pieces of art when these materials are combined. This colorful wall hanging will add a dose of warmth to any room.

Instructions on page 69

GOD'S EYE WALL HANGING

SHOWN ON PAGE 68

branches • feathers • assorted colors of yarn • wooden beads
scissors • glue • an awl or drill

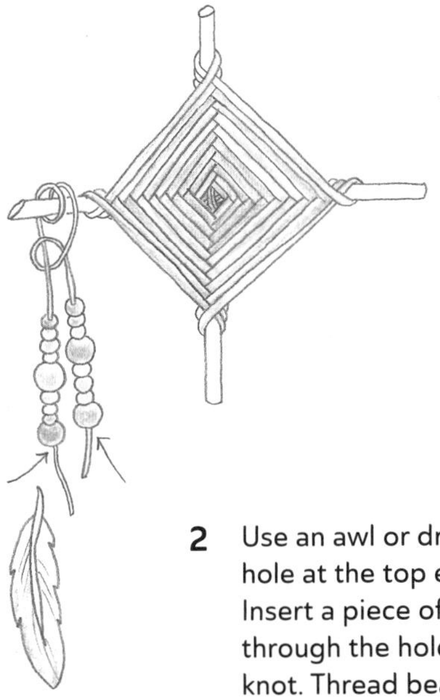

1 Follow steps 1–5 on pages 66–67 to make four God's eyes in different sizes. Use 4 in (10 cm) branches for A, 6 in (15 cm) branches for B, 8 in (20 cm) branches for C, and 10 in (25 cm) branches for D. Tie pieces of waxed twine to the horizontal branch ends on each God's eye, and embellish with beads and feathers.

2 Use an awl or drill to make a hole at the top end of B. Insert a piece of waxed twine through the hole and tie a knot. Thread beads onto the waxed twine and tie two more knots to make a hanging loop. Thread a few small beads onto each strand of waxed twine and knot to secure, as shown at right.

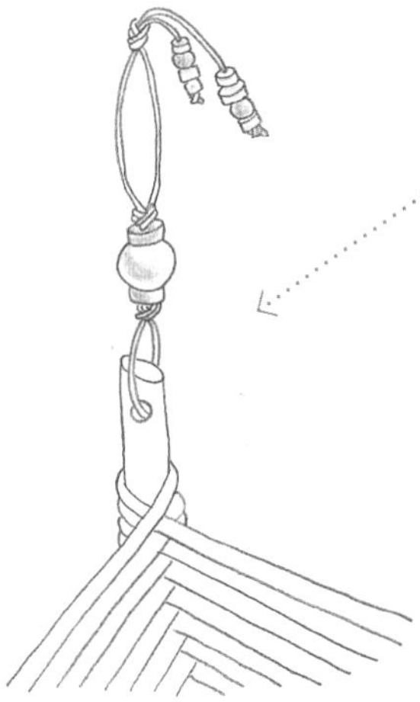

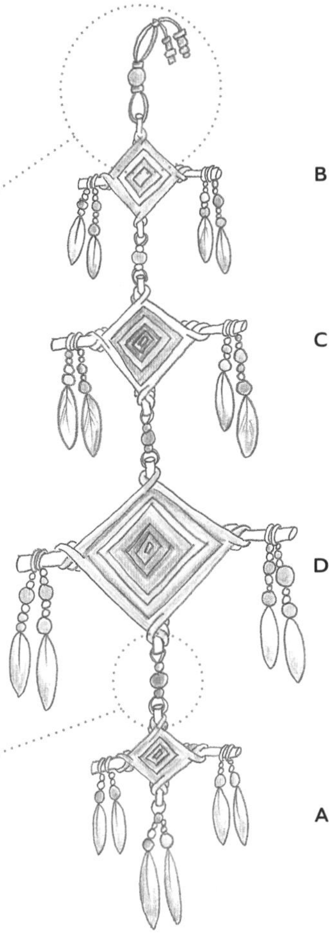

3 To assemble the wall hanging, connect the God's eyes in the following order: B, C, D, A. To connect them, make a hole at the top and the bottom of the vertical branches and tie together using waxed twine and beads, as shown at right. Tie a piece of waxed twine embellished with beads and feathers to the bottom hole of A.

THEME

8

Clarity

If you asked me to name one of the best things about living in the country, I'd say it's waking up with a clear head in the mornings. There's no need for an alarm clock when you have the birds to wake you up each morning.

Even though I throw the window open noisily, the mountain bird no longer flies away. Instead, it sits preening its feathers with great care, without noticing me and my bedhead that resembles a bird's nest.

My body becomes as light as a feather as I listen to the clear and gracious birdsong.

Image features the Bird Wreath Dream Catcher.
See page 74 for instructions.

Bird Wreath Dream Catcher

When I first saw these vines that naturally intertwine as they grow, I knew they needed to be made into a dream catcher with a colorful bird perched in the center. I carved these birds myself using a box cutter and a scrap of wood. Don't be intimidated—it's just like sharpening a pencil.

Instructions on page 74

BIRD WREATH DREAM CATCHER

SHOWN ON PAGE 72

vine • straight branch • two scraps of wood or a branch about 1¼ in (3 cm) in diameter and 3 in (8 cm) long (for bird carving) • waxed twine • assorted colors of yarn • crochet hook • tapestry needle assorted wooden and gemstone beads • box cutter or whittling knife • acrylic paint varnish • paintbrushes • scissors • glue • drill with a 2 mm bit • toothpick

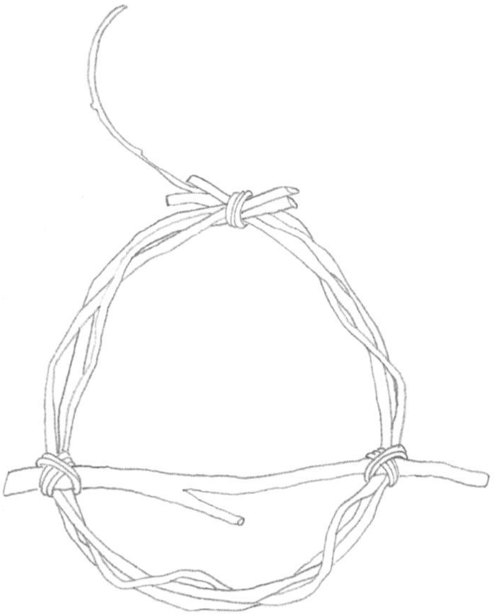

1 Bend the vines to make a circular frame about 6 in (15 cm) in diameter and secure with waxed twine. Use waxed twine to tie a straight branch across the bottom third of the frame.

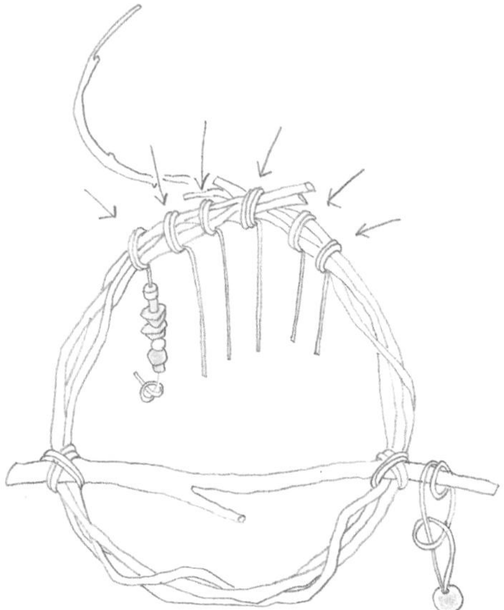

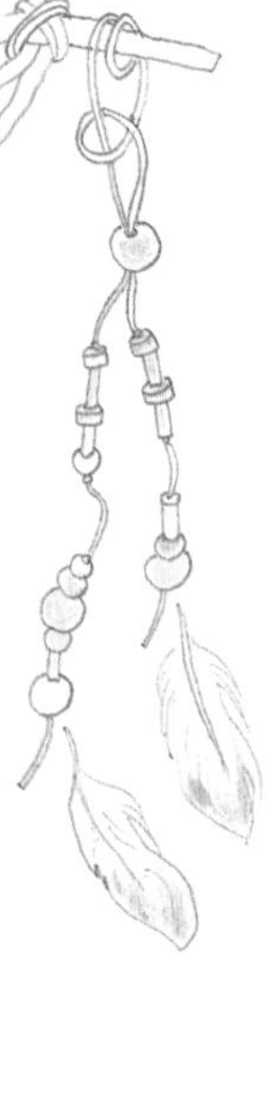

2 Tie 4 in (10 cm) pieces of waxed twine to the top of the frame at the positions indicated by the arrows. String assorted beads onto the pieces of twine. Tie pieces of waxed twine to both ends of the horizontal branch and string with beads and feathers.

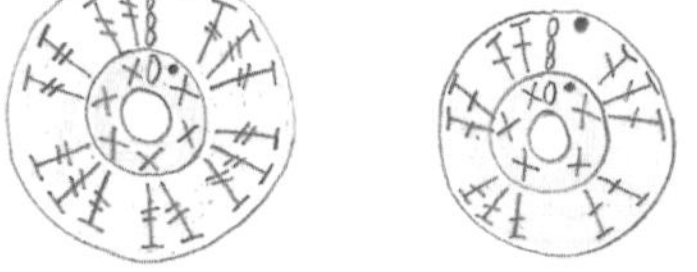

A × 1 B × 2

3 Crochet the flowers following the charts shown at left. Use pink yarn for A and white and beige yarn for B. Crochet the leaves (refer to step 5 on page 31 for the chart). Glue the crocheted flowers and leaves to the top of the frame.

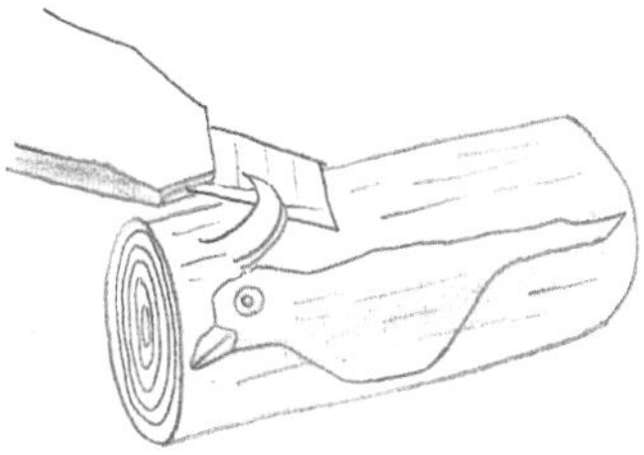

4 Sketch a bird on a scrap of wood. Use a box cutter to carefully carve the bird. Repeat to make another bird of a slightly different size.

5 Paint the birds with a variety of colors and patterns. When the paint is dry, add a coat of varnish.

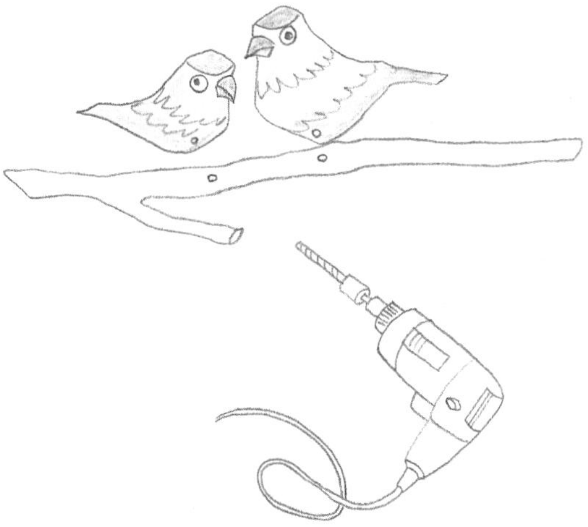

6 Use a drill to make a holes in the birds and the branch where the birds will sit. Cut the toothpick into 3/8 in (1 cm) pieces and apply glue to both ends. Insert one end into a bird and the other into the corresponding hole in the branch.

7 Crochet six circular motifs (refer to step 3 on page 102 for the chart). Make two circular motifs with 8 rounds, two with 6 rounds, and two with 4 rounds. Sew the corresponding sets together.

8 String the motifs together from largest to smallest, adding beads in between. Hang the motifs from the bottom of the circular frame. Use waxed twine and beads to create a hanging loop at the top.

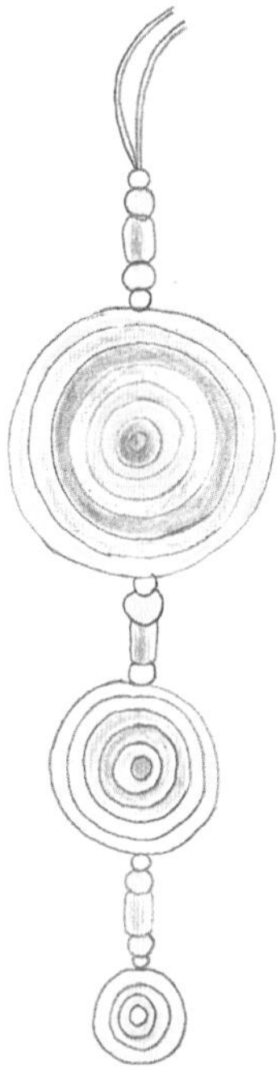

Bird Perch Dream Catcher

This design uses the same basic techniques as the dream catcher on page 72, but the semicircle frame gives it a completely different look. Although the birds featured in this collection are just rustic carvings, they look perfectly at home perched upon these branches.

Instructions on page 77

BIRD PERCH DREAM CATCHER

SHOWN ON PAGE 76

flexible branch about 12 in (30 cm) long • straight branch • scrap of wood or a branch about 1¼ in (3 cm) in diameter and 3 in (8 cm) long (for bird carving) • waxed twine assorted colors of yarn • crochet hook • tapestry needle • assorted wooden beads box cutter or whittling knife • acrylic paint • varnish • paintbrushes • scissors glue • drill with a 2 mm bit • toothpick

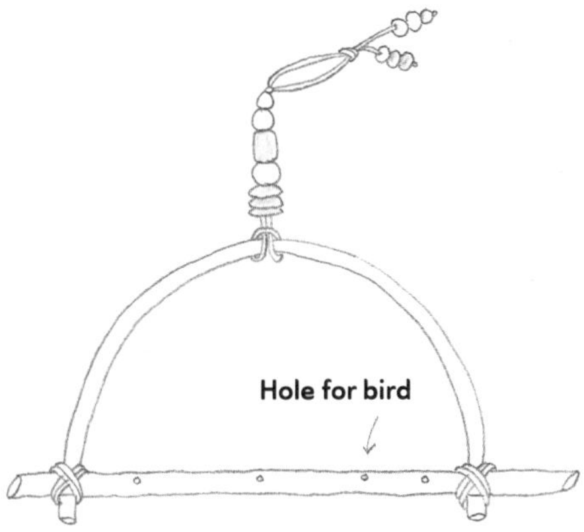

1 Bend the 12 in (30 cm) long branch to make a semicircular frame, then use waxed twine to tie the straight branch across the bottom. Use waxed twine and beads to create a hanging loop at the top of the frame. Drill four holes into the horizontal branch as shown above.

2 Insert pieces of waxed twine through the outermost holes, knot to secure, and string with beads and feathers. Crochet the circular motifs and string them together as noted in steps 7 and 8 on page 75. Insert the assembled motifs through the hole at the middle of the branch. Crochet the flowers and leaves as noted in step 3 on page 74 and glue to the left side of the semicircular frame. Make a bird and attach to the branch using toothpicks and glue as noted in steps 4–6 on page 75.

THEME

9

Nature

It's been years since I watched the movie Dances with Wolves. The details of the plot are a bit hazy, but the beautiful names of the Native American characters are still quite clear in my memory: Ten Bears, Kicking Bird, Stands with a Fist, Wind In His Hair.

I love the Native American tradition where personality, temperament, and life experiences often become names. In Native American culture, names are not just given, they are earned.

After watching the movie, I told my husband that I would love to have a name like that. So he gave me the name "Makes Beautiful Things by Hand." I love it.

Image features the Sunshine Dream Catcher.
See page 82 for instructions.

Sunshine Dream Catcher

This dream catcher is constructed from completely natural materials, including silver vine branches and beads carved from the seeds of the soapberry tree. Silver vine is known for its effectiveness in controlling insomnia and inflammation, making it an ideal material for dream catchers.

Instructions on page 82

A Note on Animism

Native Americans have always held a deep reverence for nature. As proponents of animism, Native Americans believe that everything has a spirit, even inanimate objects such as rocks, rivers, and trees. As dream catchers were made of natural materials, such as tree branches, animal bones, bird feathers, shells, and fruit, it was believed that the spirits of these objects were imbued within the dream catcher itself.

SUNSHINE DREAM CATCHER

SHOWN ON PAGE 81

vines • 5½ yards (5 m) of waxed twine • shells • beads carved from seeds
wooden tube beads • coral and gemstone beads • assorted colors of wool yarn
crochet needle • tapestry needle • scissors • glue

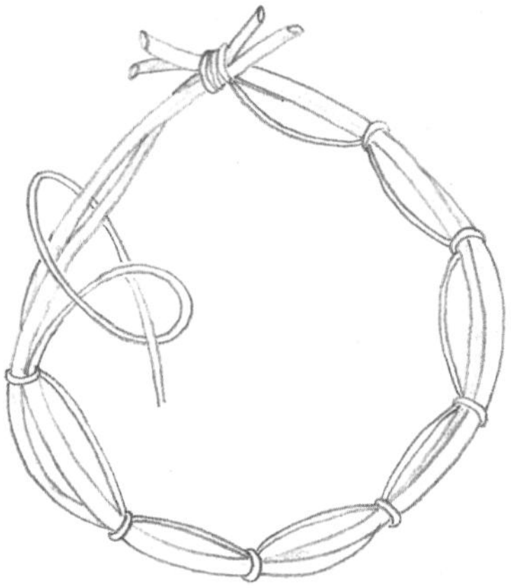

1 Allow the vine to dry out before bending it into a circular frame about 8 in (20 cm) in diameter. Secure with waxed twine, then tie the twine around the frame at equal intervals for a total of 10 loops.

2 When making the second row, tie five knots onto each loop from the first row.

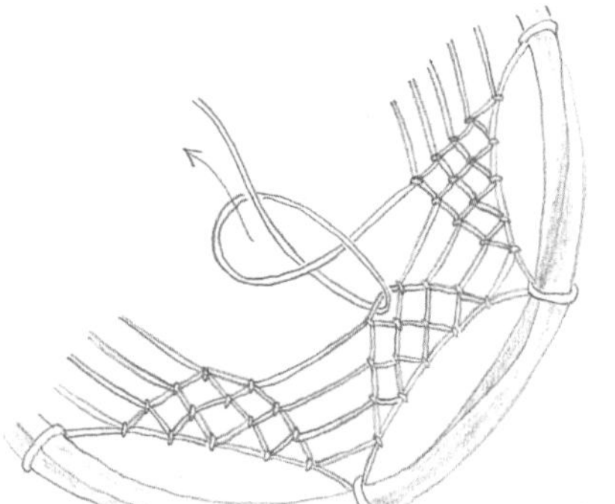

3 Follow the same process to tie four knots for each loop in the third row, three knots for each loop in the fourth row, two knots for each loop in the fifth row, and then one knot for each loop in the sixth row.

4 Follow the chart shown above to crochet a circular motif using a different color of yarn for each round. Refer to pages 140–141 for basic crochet techniques.

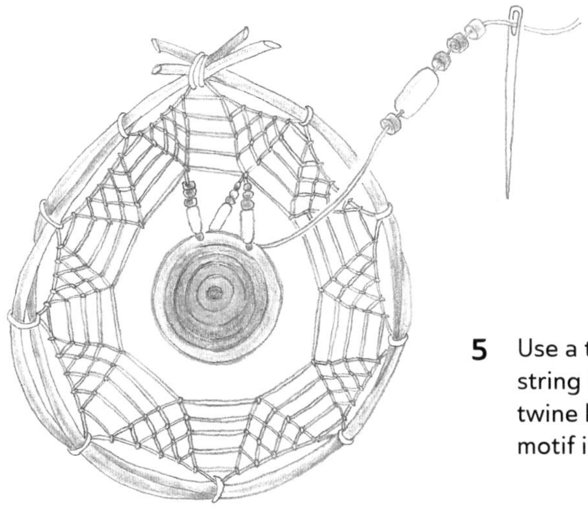

5 Use a tapestry needle and waxed twine to string beads between the woven waxed twine loops and the crocheted circular motif in a sunbeam pattern.

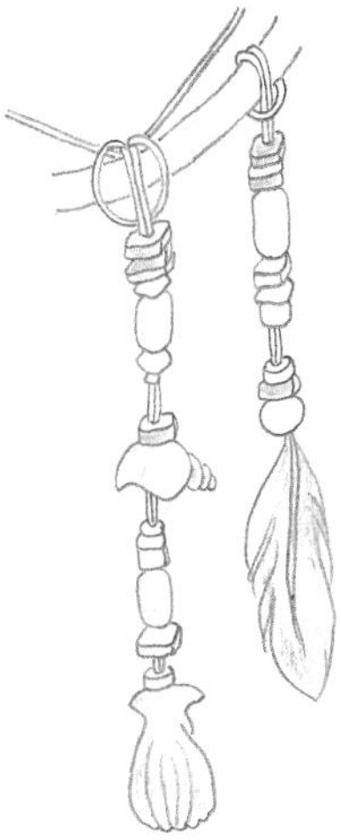

6 Cut five 16 in (40 cm) pieces of waxed twine, fold in half, and tie to the bottom of the circular frame. Thread assorted beads and shells onto the waxed twine and secure with knots, as shown at left. Glue feathers inside the holes of some of the beads if desired.

7 Cut a 12 in (30 cm) piece of waxed twine, fold in half, and tie to the top of the circular frame. Add beads and tie a knot to create a hanging loop.

Mystical Dream Catcher

This dream catcher uses the same basic design as the one on page 81, but by making a few simple changes to the materials, the finished result has a completely different look. Instead of using trendy, colorfully dyed feathers, try using naturally colored ones for a more authentic look.

Instructions on page 85

MYSTICAL DREAM CATCHER

SHOWN ON PAGE 84

vines • 5½ yards (5 m) of waxed twine • feathers
wooden tube beads • coral and gemstone beads • assorted colors of wool yarn
crochet needle • tapestry needle • scissors • glue

1 Follow steps 1–5 on pages 82–83 to make the circular frame.

2 Cut five 20 in (50 cm) pieces of waxed twine, fold in half, and tie to the bottom of the frame at the positions indicated by arrows at left.

3 Thread beads onto the strands of waxed twine and secure in place with knots. Note: Refer to the photo on the opposite page to see how the waxed twine is looped through some beads. Apply dabs of glue to the ends of the feathers and insert into the holes of the beads.

4 Make a hanging loop as shown in step 7 on page 83.

THEME

10

Heritage

After finishing fall harvest, my grandfather would spend the long winter evenings twisting straw into rope and making all sorts of useful things for life on the farm: baskets for fertilizer, seed bags, and cow muzzles to name a few. In my eyes, my grandfather was not just a farmer, but also a skilled craftsman.

Years later, making a dream catcher by weaving colorful yarn onto branches, I am reminded of my childhood and the time I spent sitting at my grandfather's side, learning how to twist straw into rope.

Images opposite and above feature the Woven Net Dream Catcher.
See page 92 for instructions.

Woven Net Dream Catcher

Weaving, or the process of interlacing threads to form fabric, has been used to create clothes, tools, and other necessities for thousands of years. Thin, yet durable yarn is strung vertically onto a Y-shaped branch, then colorful yarns are woven through to create a decorative dream catcher perfect for an empty wall or the space above a headboard. A net-like dream catcher web hangs from the lower branch and is embellished with pompoms, beads, and feathers.

Instructions on page 92

Tapestry Dream Catcher

This diminutive design features a square frame and colorfully woven tapestry at the center. Just like when painting, you can play with color, pattern, and texture by experimenting with yarn choice. This simple dream catcher is a wonderful project to make alongside children—they especially love the round, fluffy pompoms!

Instructions on page 94

WOVEN NET DREAM CATCHER

SHOWN ON PAGE 88

y-shaped branch • white cotton yarn • assorted colors and weights of yarn • tapestry needle • scissors glue • assorted wooden beads • feathers • thick paper or cardboard • suede cord

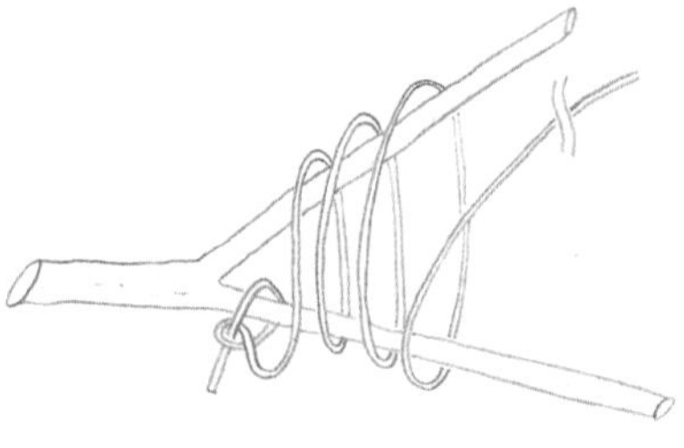

1 Wrap the white cotton yarn around the Y-shaped branch vertically, spacing the rows about 3/8 in (1 cm) apart. Pull the yarn taut as you work. The total number of rows will vary based on the size of your branch, but try to make about 20 rows.

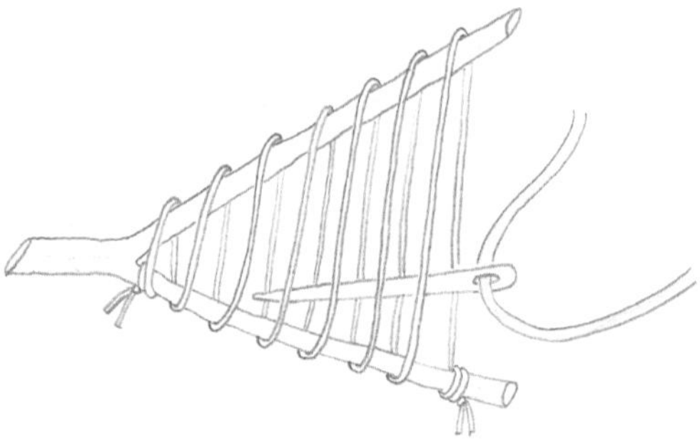

2 Thread a tapestry needle with yarn and alternately weave over and under the rows of white cotton yarn.

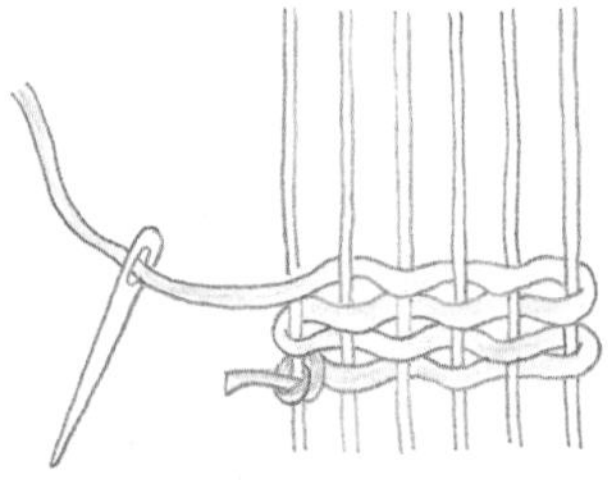

3 Weave tightly so there is no space visible between the yarn, but be careful not to alter the tension of the white cotton yarn. Change yarn as desired, securing the ends in place with knots.

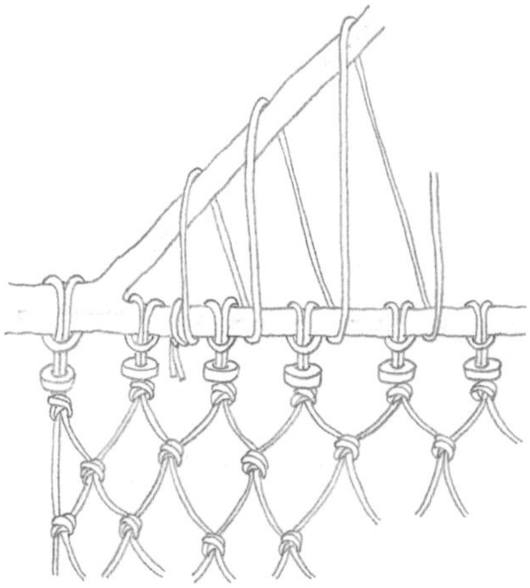

4 Cut twelve pieces of white cotton yarn, fold in half, and tie to the lower branch. Thread a bead onto each piece and tie a knot. Next, knot the pieces of white cotton yarn to form a net (refer to step 7 on page 67).

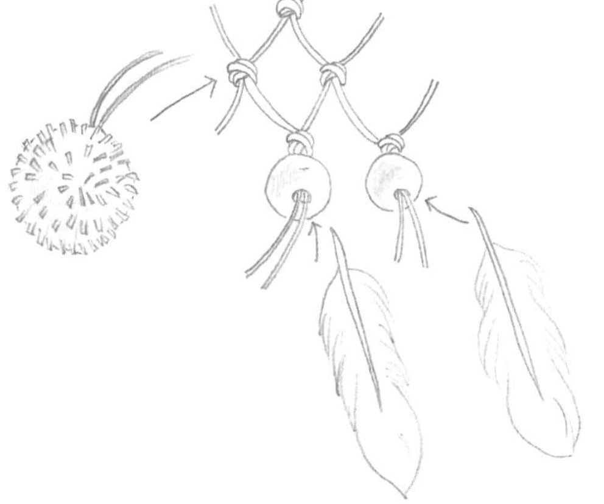

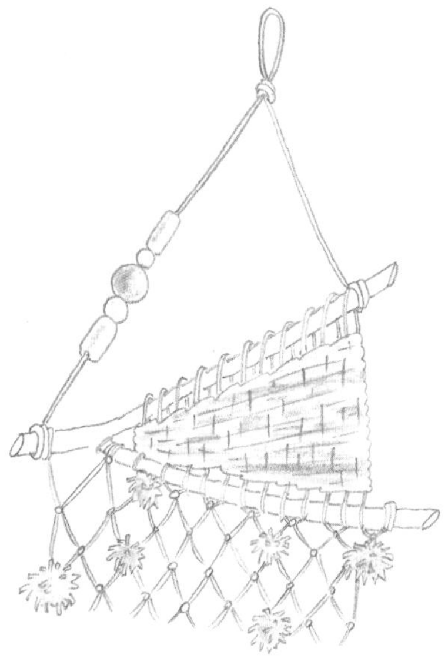

5 When the net is complete, thread a wooden bead onto the end of each piece of white cotton yarn. Apply dabs of glue to the tip of each feather and insert into the bead holes. Make pompoms as shown below and tie to the net as desired.

6 Make a hanging strap by tying suede cord strung with beads to each end of the upper branch.

HOW TO MAKE A POMPOM

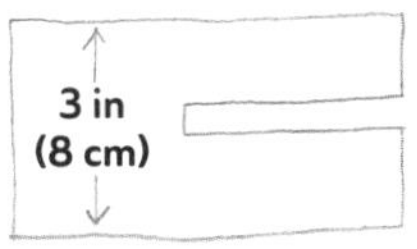

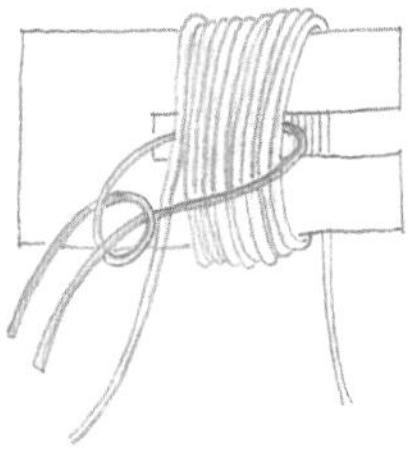

1 Cut a rectangle of thick paper or cardboard, then cut out a notch at the center as shown above.

2 Wrap with yarn (the more you wrap, the bigger and rounder the pompom). Use a single color or try multiple colors of yarn for a fun pattern. When you reach the desired size, use a piece of yarn to securely tie the bundle together at the middle.

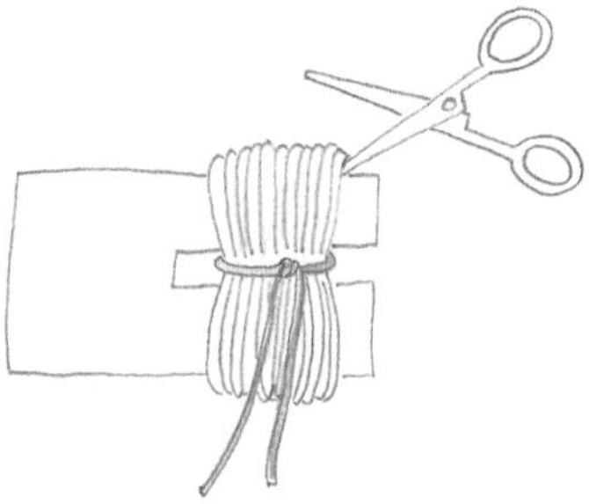

3 Cut the loops along the top and bottom.

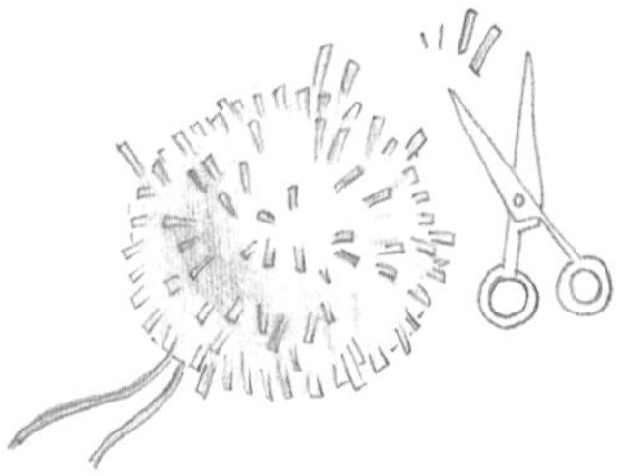

4 Trim the pompom into a round shape.

TAPESTRY DREAM CATCHER

SHOWN ON PAGE 90

four straight branches about 8 in (20 cm) long each • white cotton yarn
assorted colors and weights of yarn • tapestry needle • scissors • assorted wooden beads
thick paper or cardboard

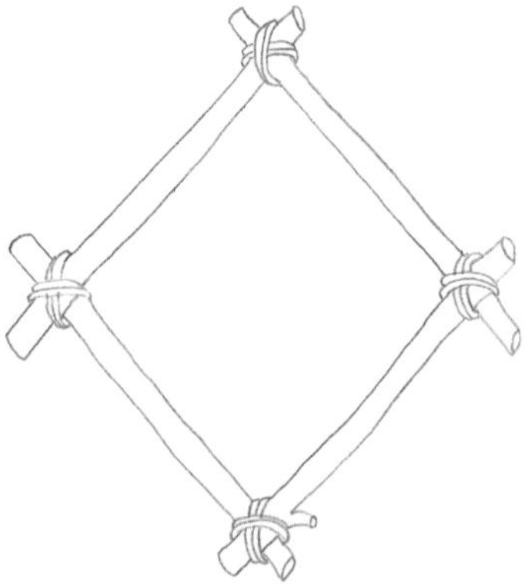

1 Make a diamond-shaped frame by overlapping the branch ends and secure in place with yarn.

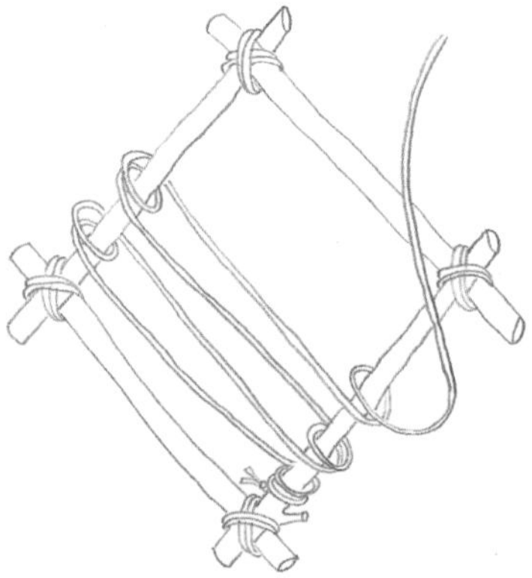

2 Wrap the white cotton yarn around the frame vertically, spacing the rows about 3/8 in (1 cm) apart. Pull the yarn taut as you work.

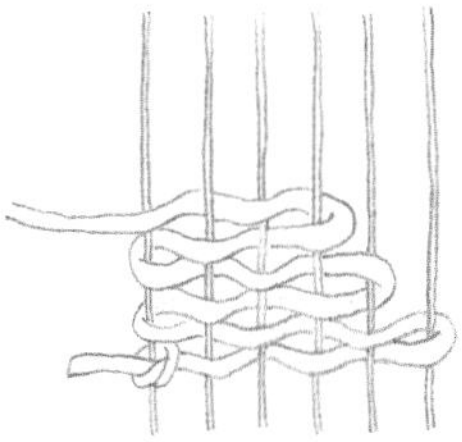

3 Thread a tapestry needle with yarn and alternately weave over and under the rows of white cotton yarn. Change yarn as desired, securing the ends in place with knots.

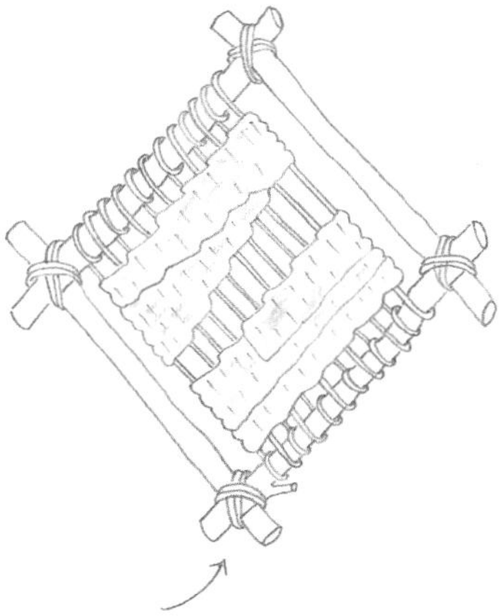

4 Fill the entire area or leave negative space to create unique patterns.

5 Make three pompoms in different colors and sizes. String them together from large to small and tie to the bottom of the frame at the position indicated by the arrow in the step 4 diagram. Use yarn and beads to create a hanging loop at the top of the frame.

THEME

11

Blessings

May the warm winds of heaven blow softly upon your house.
May the Great Spirit bless all who enter there.
May your moccasins make happy tracks in many snows.
And may the rainbow always touch your shoulder.

- Cherokee Blessing -

Image features the Dream Catcher of Hope.
See page 102 for instructions.

Dream Catcher of Hope

Rainbows grace the sky after storms and are universal symbols of hope and fresh starts. This rainbow dream catcher is a perfect gift for someone going through a difficult time. It is made from a forsythia branch, which represents anticipation in the language of flowers, and features a crocheted rainbow woven into the center of the web.

Instructions on page 102

Shades of Green Dream Catcher

This variation celebrates all the lush shades of green found in nature. It uses a green branch from a wild rose-bush for the frame and features several colors of green yarn and beads for a soft, peaceful impression.

Instructions on page 103

DREAM CATCHER OF HOPE

SHOWN ON PAGE 98

forsythia branch • waxed twine • circular wooden beads • white wooden tube beads assorted colors of yarn to make a rainbow • crochet hook • tapestry needle • scissors

1 Bend the branch to make a circular frame about 8 in (20 cm) in diameter and secure with waxed twine. Use the waxed twine to tie 24 loops to the frame (refer to step 3 on page 20).

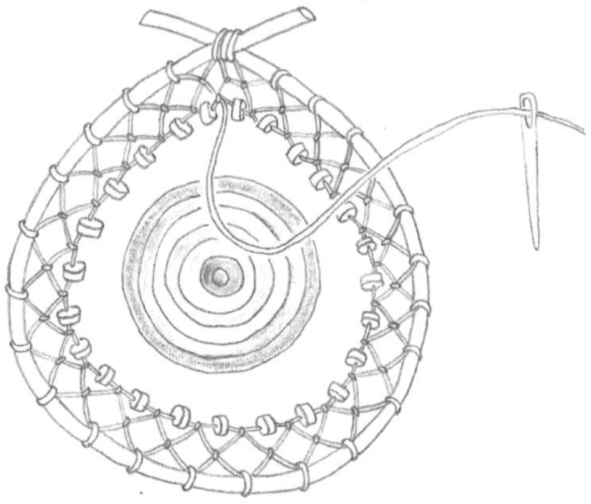

2 Weave two more rows, adding white wooden tube beads to the third row (refer to steps 4 and 5 on page 20). Do not cut the waxed twine—you'll use it to sew the crocheted motif to the center in step 4.

3 Crochet the circular motif following the chart above. Use a different color of yarn for each round to form a rainbow.

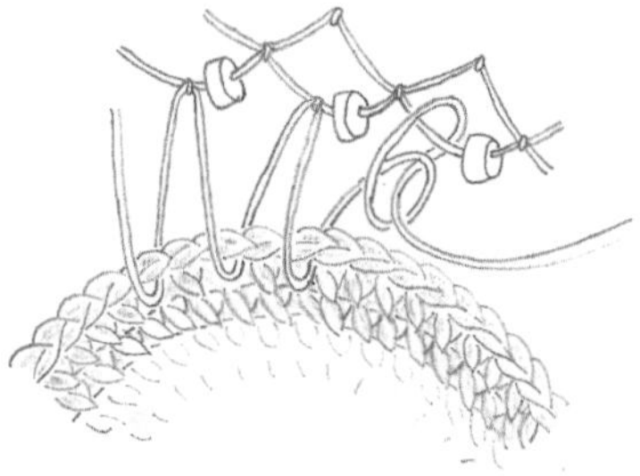

4 Weave the fourth row, using a tapestry needle to sew the waxed twine through the crocheted motif every two stitches, then tie to a loop.

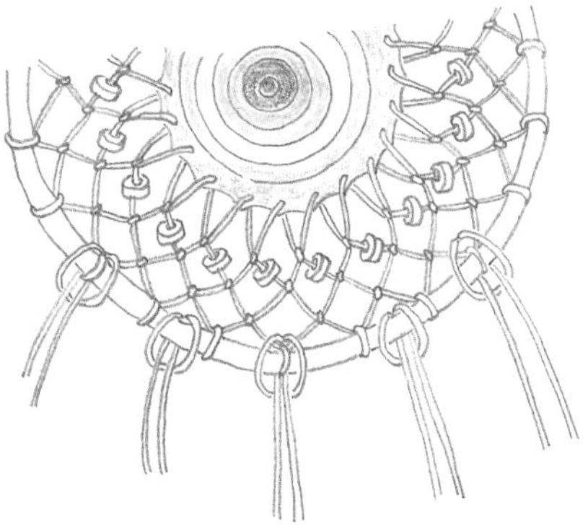

5 Cut five pieces of waxed twine, fold in half, and tie to the bottom of the frame.

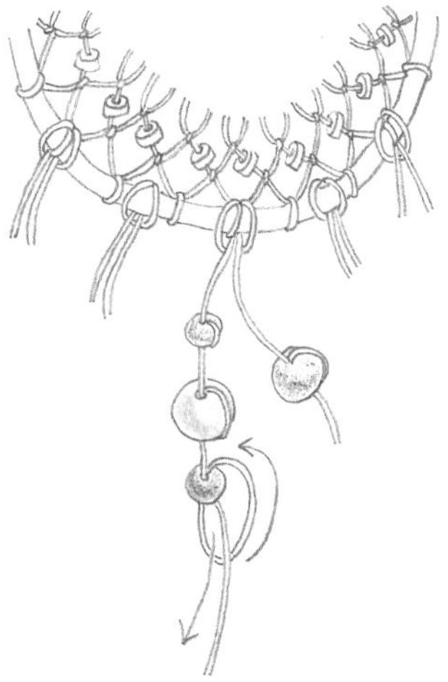

6 String assorted colors and sizes of wooden beads onto the pieces of waxed twine. Thread the waxed twine through the wooden beads as shown above to securely attach them and hold them in place.

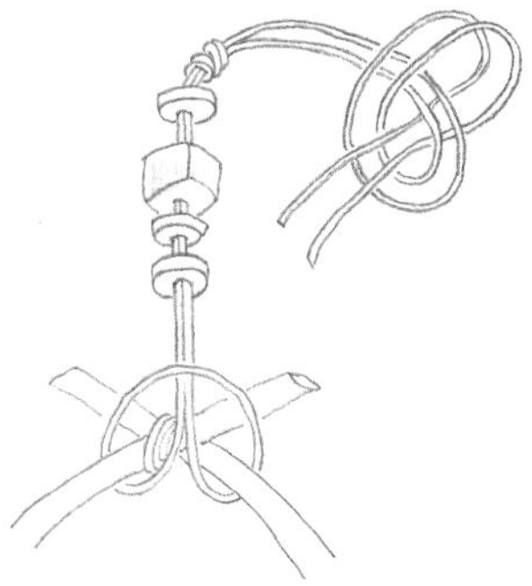

7 Cut a 12 in (30 cm) piece of waxed twine, fold in half, and tie to the top of the frame. String with assorted beads and tie knots to make a hanging loop.

SHADES OF GREEN DREAM CATCHER

SHOWN ON PAGE 100

wild rosebush branch • waxed twine • green circular wooden beads • assorted green shades of yarn crochet hook • tapestry needle • scissors

Follow the instructions for the Dream Catcher of Hope on page 102 and above, but use green yarn and beads. Tie three pieces of waxed twine to the bottom of the frame instead of five.

THEME

12

Health

The day my son was born, my mother hung a geumjul across the entrance of my apartment. In Korea, a geumjul is a straw garland hung across a gate upon the birth of a child to prevent evil spirits from entering the house.

"Mom, no one believes in these things anymore," I grumbled, but inside, I felt slightly relieved. As a new mother, I welcomed all the help I could get.

When a close friend recently had a baby, I made a dream catcher mobile to hang above the baby's crib. I wanted to create something beautiful for the baby to look at and wished for her to grow up strong and healthy.

Image features the Dream Catcher Mobile.
See page 110 for instructions.

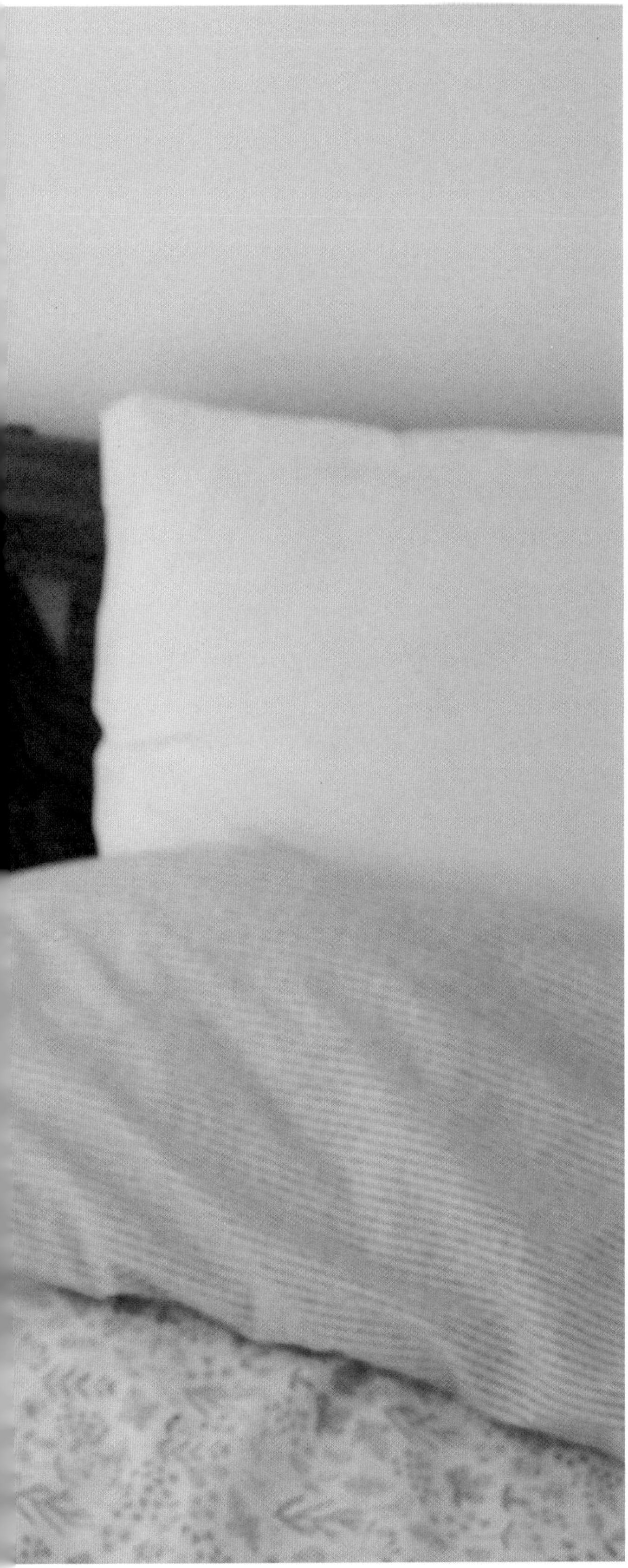

Dream Catcher Mobile

In addition to being pretty to look at, mobiles are excellent for development because they spin around and stimulate a baby's curiosity. Rather than buying a store-bought mobile, try making one from natural materials. Since this dream catcher is designed for a baby and it's important to keep safety in mind, it features lovely pastel tones of soft yarn rather than beads and feathers.

Instructions on page 110

Pyramid Dream Catcher Mobile

Three different size dream catcher frames are layered vertically to create a uniquely-shaped mobile. Colorful crochet motifs, beads, and feathers add a whimsical touch.

Instructions on page 113

DREAM CATCHER MOBILE

SHOWN ON PAGE 106

branches • waxed twine • cotton or wool yarn in lemon, pink, white, light green, sky blue, and beige stuffing • crochet hook • tapestry needle • thick paper or card stock

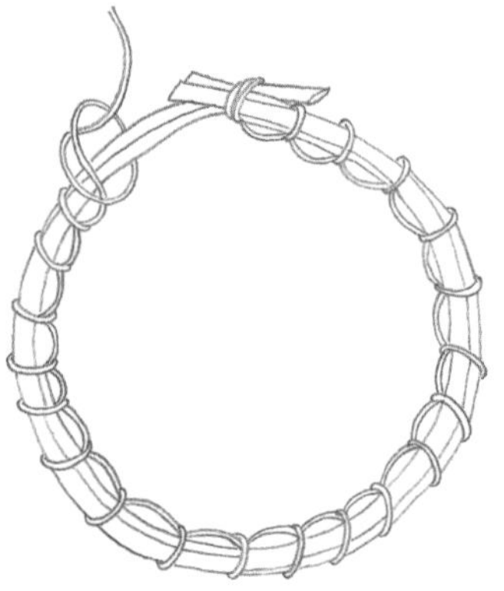

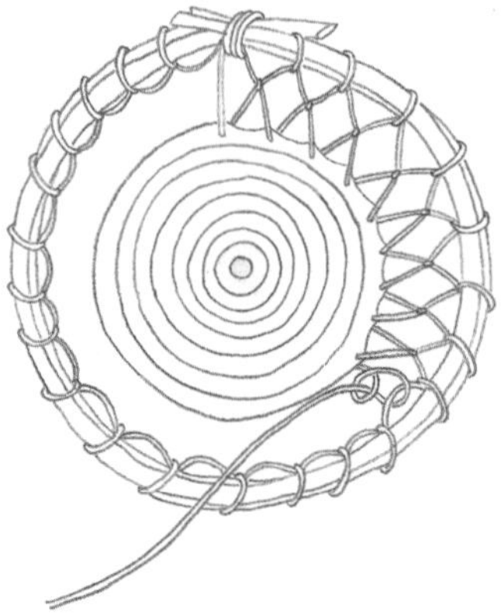

1 Bend the branch to make a circular frame about 8 in (20 cm) in diameter and secure with waxed twine. Use the waxed twine to tie 24 loops around the frame (refer to step 3 on page 20). Do not cut the waxed twine.

2 Crochet the circular motif following the chart on page 102, but use the following color order: lemon, beige, light green, sky blue, pink, white, beige, light green, sky blue. Weave the second row, using a tapestry needle to sew the waxed twine through the crocheted motif every two stitches, then tie to a loop (refer to step 4 on page 102).

3 Make six tassels (refer to page 111), six crocheted balls (refer to page 112), and 12 pompoms (refer to pages 93–94) in assorted colors and tie in place to secure. String a crocheted ball and two pompoms onto each tassel.

4 Tie the tassels to the frame at different heights to create variety. Next, tie five strands of yarn to the frame and gather together at the top. Make a knot to form a hanging loop.

5 Crochet four circular motifs (refer to step 3 on page 102 for the chart). Make two circular motifs with 6 rounds and two with 8 rounds. Sew the corresponding sets together. Tie the crocheted motifs together vertically and use a tapestry need to sew to the center of the dream catcher.

HOW TO MAKE A TASSEL

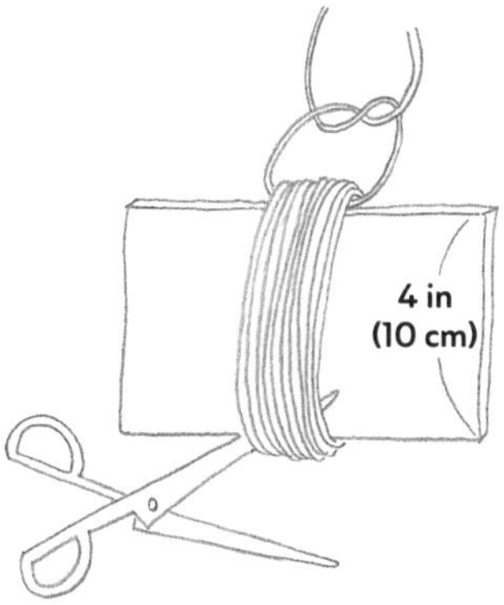

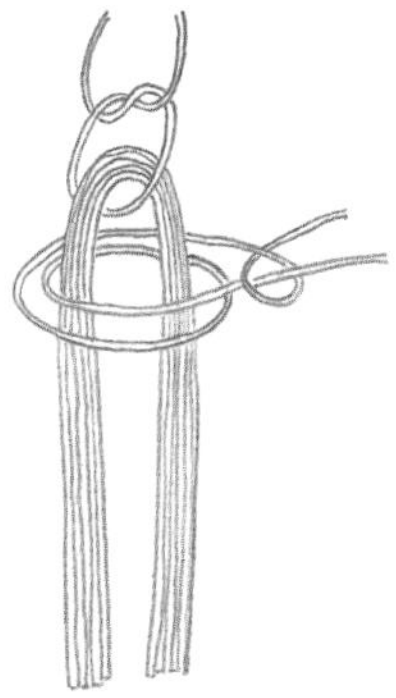

1 Wrap yarn around a 4 in (10 cm) wide piece of thick paper or card stock (the more you wrap, the bigger the tassel). Securely tie the wraps together at the top. Cut the loops along the bottom.

2 Wrap a piece of yarn around the bundle twice, about 5/8 in (1.5 cm) from the top and tie in place to secure.

HOW TO MAKE A CROCHETED BALL

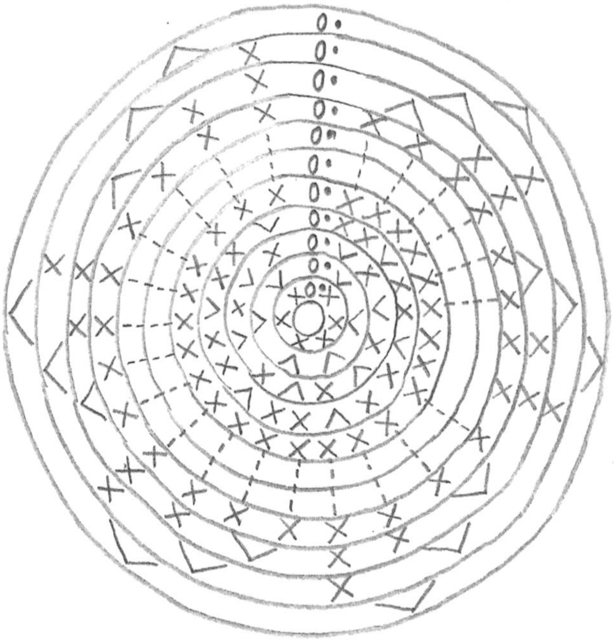

Round 1: Start with a slip knot ring. Work 6 single crochet into the center of the ring. Join with a slip stitch. (6 stitches)

Round 2: Chain 1. *2 single crochet in the next stitch. Repeat from *. Join with a slip stitch. (12 stitches)

Round 3: Chain 1. *Single crochet. 2 single crochet in the next stitch. Repeat from *. Join with a slip stitch. (18 stitches)

Round 4: Chain 1. *Single crochet, single crochet, 2 single crochet in the next stitch. Repeat from *. Join with a slip stitch. (24 stitches)

Round 5: Chain 1. Single crochet in every stitch. Join with a slip stitch. (24 stitches)

Round 6: Chain 1. Single crochet in every stitch. Join with a slip stitch. (24 stitches)

Round 7: Chain 1. Single crochet in every stitch. Join with a slip stitch. (24 stitches)

Round 8: Chain 1. Single crochet in every stitch. Join with a slip stitch. (24 stitches)

Round 9: Chain 1. *Single crochet, single crochet, single crochet 2 together. Repeat from *. Join with a slip stitch. (18 stitches)

Round 10: Chain 1. *Single crochet, single crochet 2 together. Repeat from *. Join with a slip stitch. (12 stitches)

Round 11: Chain 1. *Single crochet 2 together. Repeat from *. Join with a slip stitch. (6 stitches).

Fill the ball with stuffing. Use a tapestry needle to insert the yarn tail through the remaining 6 stitches and pull the opening closed.

★You can make a different size crocheted balls by starting with 7 or 8 stitches instead of 6. The crochet method is same, just change the number of repeats accordingly.

PYRAMID DREAM CATCHER MOBILE

SHOWN ON PAGE 108

branches • waxed twine • assorted colors of yarn • crochet hook • tapestry needle assorted wooden beads • feathers • scissors • glue

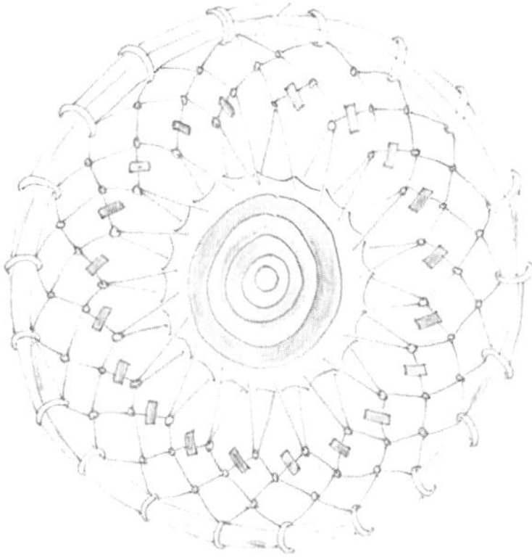

1 Crochet three circular motifs in different sizes and colors (refer to step 3 on page 102 for the chart). Bend the branches to make three frames based on the size of the crocheted motifs. Make the dream catcher webs as shown in steps 1–4 on page 102.

2 Use waxed twine strung with beads to tie the frames together vertically, with the largest frame positioned on the bottom and the smallest frame positioned on the top. Make a hanging loop at the top. Tie pieces of waxed twine to the bottom frame and string with beads and feathers.

THEME

13

Serenity

As I sit on the sofa with a cup of coffee in hand and stare at the green plants hanging by the window, I feel instantly refreshed. I'm struck with the idea to combine dream catchers and plants for a double dose of natural beauty.

Image features the Air Plant Dream Catcher.
See page 120 for instructions.

RBAN
UNGLE

Air Plant Dream Catcher

Combine plants known for purifying the air with a dream catcher to block negative vibes—a match made in heaven! We used fishing line to attach Xerographica, Ionantha, and the elegant Andreana to the frame of this dream catcher.

Instructions on page 120

Plant Hanger Dream Catcher

It's a shame to throw away empty jars after you finish the contents. When I come across prettily shaped jars, I like to repurpose them into useful plant hangers. Add a small dream catcher or two for a special touch.

Instructions on page 122

C
IGOR JOSIF
JUDITH DE G
URBAN
JUNGLE
LIVING AND STYLING
WITH PLANTS

AIR PLANT DREAM CATCHER

SHOWN ON PAGE 116

vine • white cotton yarn • crochet hook • tapestry needle • feathers • clear fishing line assorted wooden beads • scissors • air plants • glue

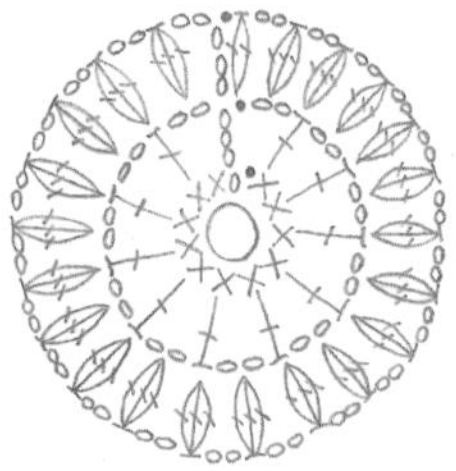

1 Crochet the circular motif with white cotton yarn following the chart above.

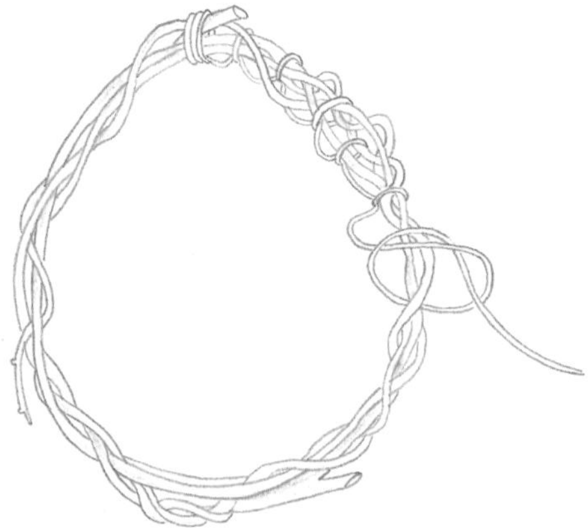

2 Bend the vine to make a circular frame about 9 3/4 in (25 cm) in diameter and secure with white cotton yarn. Use the yarn to tie 22 loops around the frame (refer to step 2 on page 20).

3 Weave two more rows (refer to step 3 on page 20). Do not cut the yarn. Position the crochet motif from step 1 at the center of the frame. Use a tapestry needle to sew the white cotton yarn to the crochet motif, then tie it to the loops (refer to step 5 page 123).

4 Use yarn and beads to make a hanging loop at the top of the frame at the positions marked by the arrows. Cut five pieces of yarn and tie them to the bottom of the frame at the positions indicated by arrows. String beads onto each strand and glue a feather to the end.

5 Arrange the air plants on the left side of the frame. Use clear fishing line to secure them in place.

Xerographica

Ionantha

Andreana

PLANT HANGER DREAM CATCHER

SHOWN ON PAGE 118

glass jar • linen yarn in white and beige • crochet hook • tapestry needle • assorted wooden beads branches • waxed twine • white cotton yarn • scissors • plants or greenery

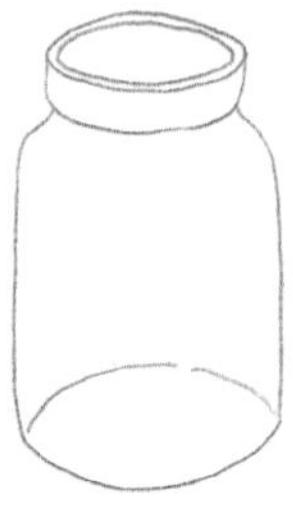

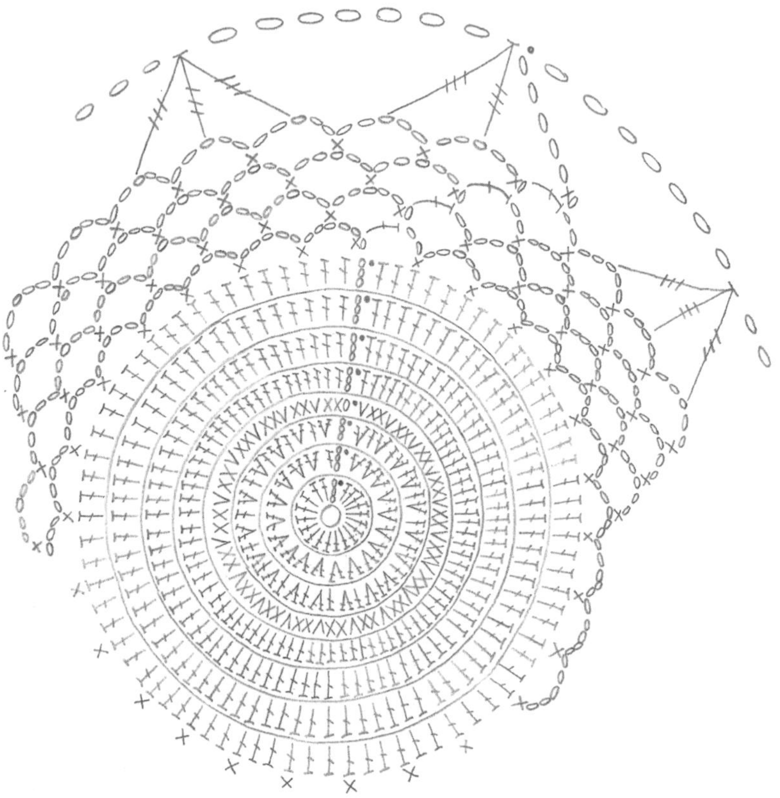

1 Clean out a glass jar. The one used here is approximately 4 in (10 cm) in diameter and 6¾ in (17 cm) tall.

2 Use the linen yarn to crochet the jar holder following the chart shown at right. Rounds 1–4 will form the bottom of the jar holder and round 5 onward will form the sides. Use beige yarn for rounds 1–7 and white yarn for round 8 onward.

3 Use chain stitch to crochet the hanging strap. Adjust the length as desired. Add beads and make a knot to secure.

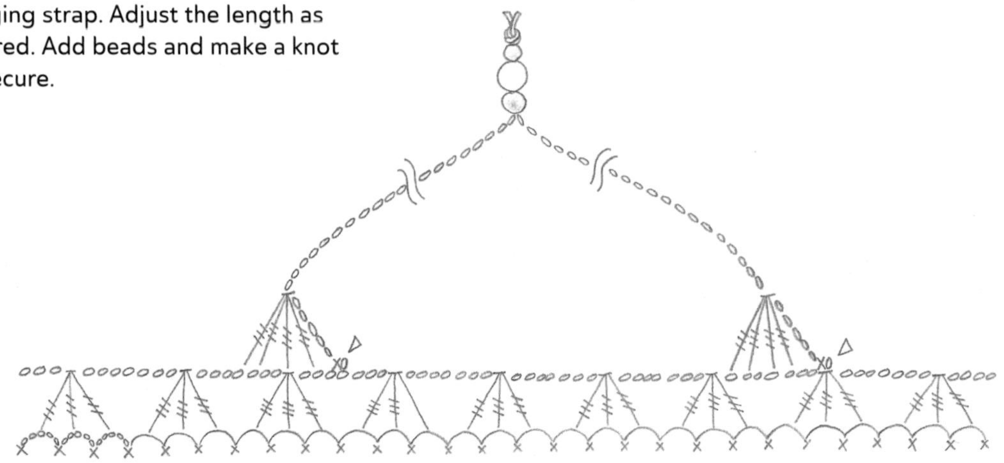

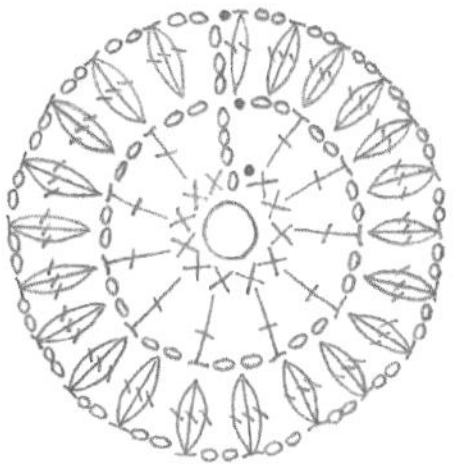

A

B

4 Use white cotton yarn to crochet circular motifs A and B following the charts shown at left.

5 Bend a branch to make a circular frame about 4 in (10 cm) in diameter. Use white cotton yarn to make the web and attach motif A as shown at left (also refer to steps 2 and 3 on page 20).

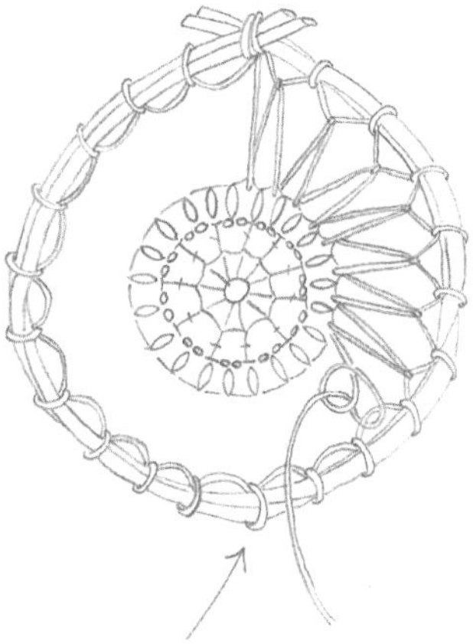

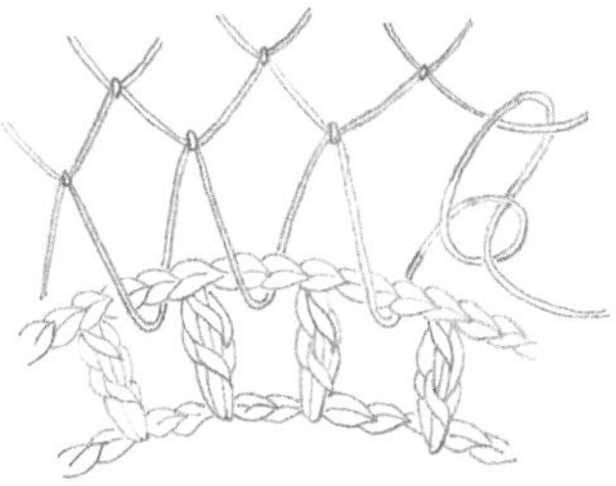

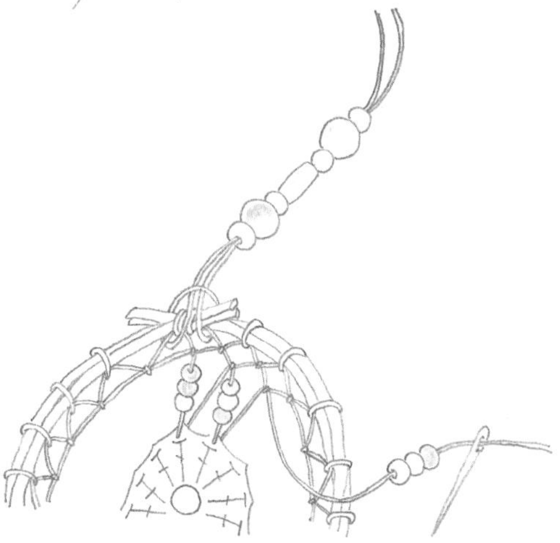

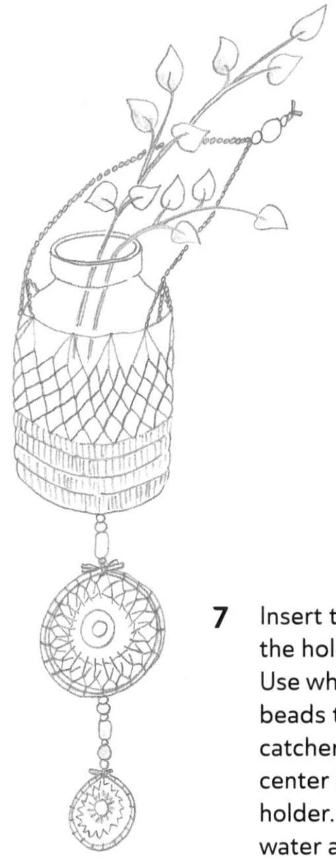

6 Bend the branch to make a circular frame about 2 in (5 cm) in diameter. Use white cotton yarn to make the web and attach motif B and beads as shown above (also refer to steps 2 and 3 on page 20). Use white cotton yarn and beads to tie the two dream catchers together at the position indicated by the arrow in the step 5 diagram.

7 Insert the glass jar into the holder made in step 3. Use white cotton yarn and beads to tie the dream catcher pendant to the center bottom of the jar holder. Fill the jar with water and add a plant or some greenery.

Inspiration Gallery

My grandparents' house had the most wonderful garden just outside the kitchen door. It had a well with cold, refreshing water, a shed with all sorts of unique treasures, persimmon trees, and beautiful peonies, cranberry bushes, and garden balsams. As a young child, this place was the best playground in the entire world and full of special memories.

Ever since then, I dreamed of having a garden just like that when I grew up. It wasn't until my own children were nearly adults themselves that I finally moved into a house with a garden of my very own. It may be small, but this garden is my happy place where I find inspiration for my work.

God's Eye Wall Hanging *page 69*

Vertical Net Dream Catcher *page 39*

LEFT: Woven Net Dream Catcher *page 92*
RIGHT: Tapestry Dream Catcher *page 94*

Woven Net Dream Catcher *page 92*

Air Plant Dream Catcher *page 120*

Dream Catcher Mobile *page 110*

God's Eye Wall Hanging *page 69*

God's Eye *page 66*

Mystical Dream Catcher *page 85*

Pyramid Dream Catcher Mobile *page 113*

Sea Glass Dream Catcher *page 46*

Vertical Net Dream Catcher *page 39*

Triangle Dream Catcher *page 38*

Crochet Stitch Guide

A few of the projects in this book use crochet to create floral embellishments or colorful circles at the center of the dream catcher webs. The following guide includes some basic crochet stitches used to create these design elements.

Slip Knot Ring

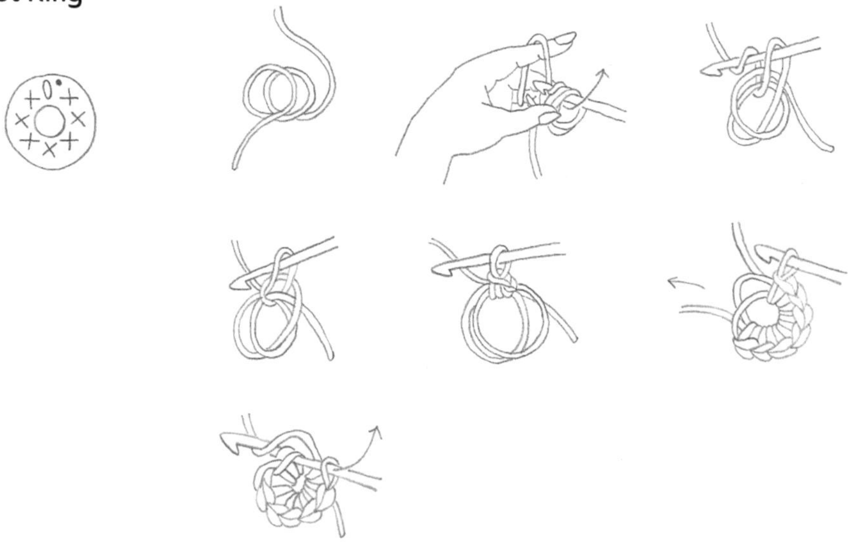

Single Crochet

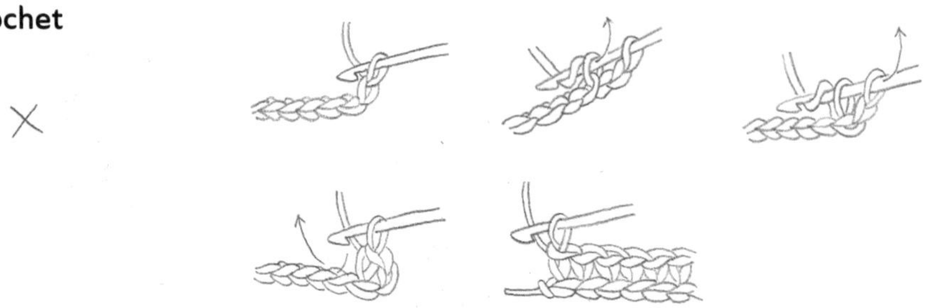

Single Crochet Increase

*Noted as ∨ in crochet charts

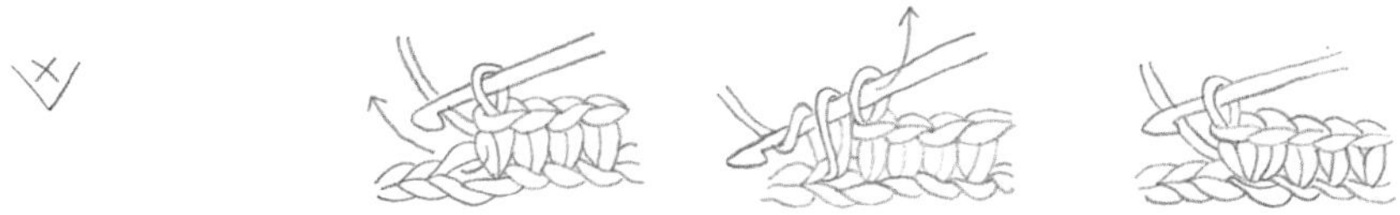

Single Crochet Decrease

*Noted as ∧ in crochet charts

Double Crochet

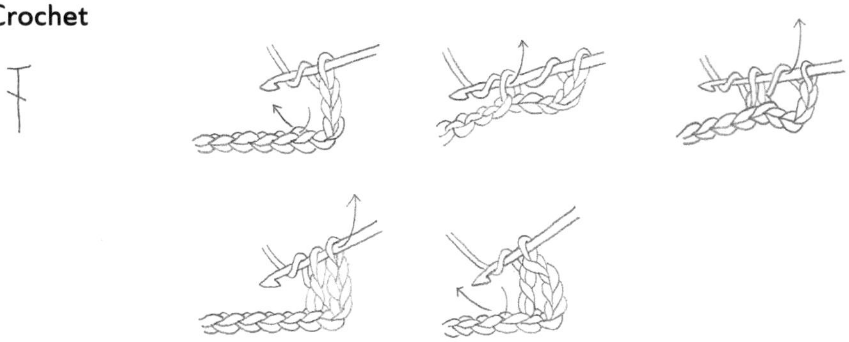

Triple Crochet

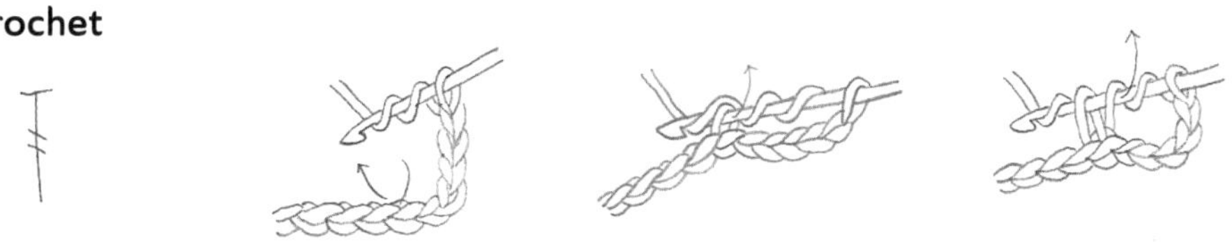

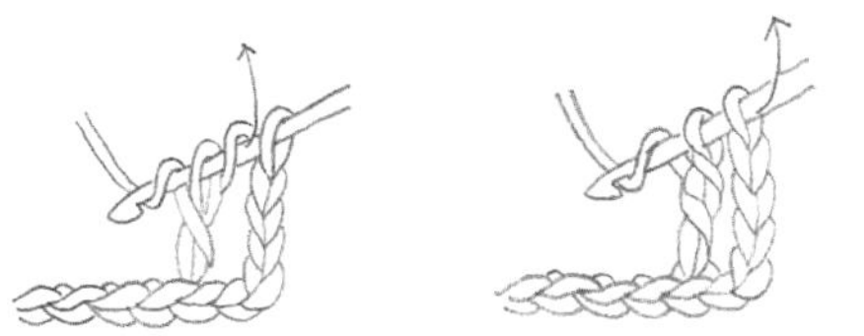

 = Double Triple Crochet

Uses the same process as triple crochet, but the yarn is wound around the crochet hook three times in step 1.

3 Double Crochet Bobble

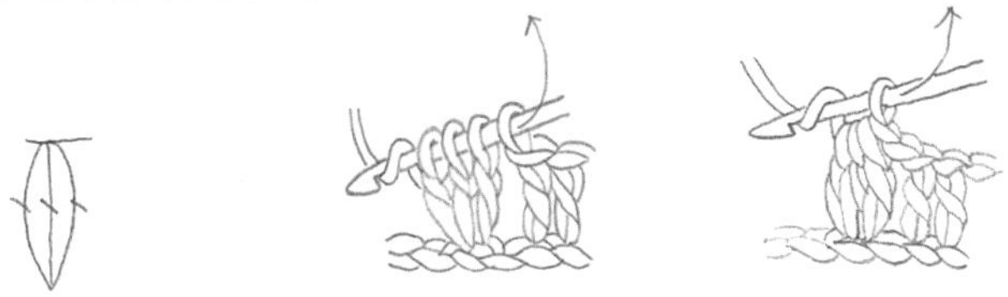

Resources

Although the majority of materials you'll need to make dream catchers can be found in nature, you may need to purchase some of the decorative elements at craft supply stores. The following stores are sources for natural materials:

Etsy
www.etsy.com
Excellent source for unique natural materials, including twine, feathers, beads, driftwood, sea glass, and seashells.

Fire Mountain Gems
www.firemountaingems.com
Online shop with an extensive selection of beads, including wood and nut beads, gemstone beads, shell beads, and more.

M&J Trimming
www.mjtrim.com
Offers an assortment of ribbon, lace, cord, and other trims

Moonlight Feather
www.moonlightfeather.com
Online shop with a wide variety of natural feathers, including peacock, ostrich, pheasant, and more.

WEBS
www.yarn.com
Known as America's yarn store, WEBS offers a broad selection of yarn in natural fibers, such as cotton, wool, and linen.

About the Author

After years of city living, Young-Ran Lee moved to the country in order to spend more time among the trees and mountains. Inspired by the beauty of her surroundings, she began combining materials from nature with crochet, weaving, and macramé to create one-of-a-kind dream catchers. Initially intended as gifts for her children, Young-Ran's dream catchers received interest and attention from others, inspiring her to share her passion. She holds regular workshops for students of all ages and gives lectures to teach about the culture and history of dream catchers. Follow her on Instagram @mari_atelier_